jerome robbins

that broadway man

that ballet man

Christine Conrad

Booth-Clibborn Editions

First published in 2000 by
Booth-Clibborn Editions
12 Percy Street
London W1T 1DW
www.booth-clibborn.com

Copyright © 2000 Christine Conrad

Design: J. Abbott Miller, Jeremy Hoffman
         Pentagram, New York
Editor: Deborah Artman

Front cover: photograph by Robert McAfee/The Jerome
Robbins Collection, The New York Public Library
Back cover: photograph by Martha Swope/TimePix

A Cataloguing-in-Publication record for this book is
available from the Publisher.

ISBN 1-86154-173-2

Printed in Korea
October 2000
First Edition

TABLE OF CONTENTS

ACKNOWLEDGMENTS

First and foremost, my grateful thanks to the Estate of Jerome Robbins, for enthusiastically supporting my work on this project through its various metamorphoses and for providing access to the vast Robbins archives: Executors Floria V. Lasky, Esq. and Allen Greenberg; Trustees Daniel N. Stern and Bill Earle, who gave generously of their time and attention and made it possible for me to include the important material from the private journals; Aidan Mooney, always there with friendship and the most excellent advice; Nadia Stern, for her warm concern and friendship; and Christopher Pennington, who as Administrator of the Robbins Foundation provided logistical help beyond measure and the benefit of his good judgment.

To Sonia Cullinen, for generously sharing her early memories and photographs.

To Fay Greenbaum, who worked with me every step of the way as researcher and whose special abilities proved invaluable. Her memories of her time as a Robbins' assistant were a particular added benefit.

To Kamal Madjidi, for his great love and support.

To Amanda Vaill, who in the course of this project became my most trusted sounding board and treasured friend.

To Deborah Jowitt, for the benefit of her wide expertise on dance and her generous spirit.

To Kathy Eldon, my dear friend, who supports me in every way.

For their brilliant design work, J. Abbott Miller, John Porter and Jeremy Hoffman of Pentagram Design, and photographer John Halpern, who did an exceptional job with the difficult task of photographing the personal journals, documents and photographs in the New York Public Library.

To my publisher Edward Booth-Clibborn, editor Deborah Artman and, in the U.K., Vicky Hayward and Denny Hemming, for their attention to excellence which shines through these pages.

To Madeleine Nichols, who supported this project from its inception; Phil Karg, who handled my large photograph requests swiftly and efficiently and with wonderful humor; Jan Schmidt, Dorothy Lourdou, Patricia Rader, Monica Moseley, Jan Schmidt, Alice Standin, Myron Switzer and the entire staff at the Dance Division of the New York Public Library. To Bob Taylor, Jeremy Megraw, Brian O'Connell and the entire staff at the Billy Rose Theater Collection of the New York Public Library, all of whom gave me excellent help. To Tom Lisanti and the entire annex staff of the New York Public Library Copy Services, especially Eydie Wiggins, Earl Poyser, Caleb Cadet and Andrea Felder.

To everyone at New York City Ballet, especially Debbie Koolish, who worked her magic everywhere.

For their additional help with research: Peter Filardo and Erika Gottfriend of the Tamiment Institute Library at New York University; Christopher Wilson at the Dramatists Guild; The New York Historical Society; Craig Urquhart of The Amberson Group; and Mark Horowitz of the Library of Congress.

Thanks to the photographers whose wonderful work is the soul of this book: Martha Swope, Eileen Darby, Costas Cacaroukas, Steven Caras, Paul Kolnik and Dominique Nabokov, as well as Jane and Steve Bellow of the Halsman Estate, Tom Gilbert of the Time-Life Picture Collection, Kathryn S. Goren of the Lewis Goren Estate, Margaret Fehl of the Fred Fehl Estate, Ronald Mandelbaum of Photofest, Eric Young of Archive Photos, Michele Hernandez of Black Star, Jennifer Bikel of Fairchild Publications and the folks at Corbis.

I'd like to thank the staff at Tower 58, where I lived for eight months and who provided important service to smooth my work. To officers James Allen and Mike Sheehan of the Midtown North Police Precinct. And special personal thanks to: Donald Saddler, Tanaquil Le Clercq, Sondra Lee, Humphrey Burton, Greg Lawrence, Phillip Sandor, Jerome Weidman, Karen Bernstein, Peter Stone, George and Shirley Perle, Martin Jarvis and Rosalind Ayres, Robert Maiorano, Helene Fields, Lili Root and the Susan Magrino Agency, and last but not least, my exceptional agent Jane Dystel and my equally exceptional lawyer Renee Schwartz, who navigated me smoothly through the transatlantic contract negotiations.

AUTHOR'S NOTE

My friendship with Jerome Robbins spanned over thirty years. In that time, I came to know a deeply complex man with great passions and equally great fears and a mountain of contradictions. This book can in no way be a full portrait, and it is of course imbued with my personal view of him. But because I was able to see the more personal side of Jerome Robbins' struggle to create, I hope to open a window of understanding to this singular artist. In the coming years, biographers will explore his life and work in greater detail, giving him the attention he is due for the magnitude of his contribution to theater, film and ballet.

To give you a sense of his voice, both the personal and public man, I have chosen to narrate the book using Robbins' own words culled from his interviews over sixty years. In these interviews, Robbins applied the same level of perfectionism to what he said about his work as he did to the work itself. There is remarkably little fat in his remarks, just as he would allow little fat in his theater and ballet work or in how he lived his life, for that matter. Everything was pared down to the most essential parts.

In the best way I know how, and as heartfelt homage to all the delight Jerome Robbins gave to the world, it has been my deepest aim to create a book that is a delight to the mind, the eye and the soul.

New York, May 2000

INTRODUCTION

"Look, I hate … big statements about dance. Essentially what I care about is working, that's what I feel my job is. I don't want to fall into profundities and artistry and surround everything with whipped cream. I work, only instead of being a plumber, I'm a choreographer."

For the whole of his life, Jerome Robbins *worked.* From earliest childhood to his last drop of energy, he never stopped. If work was his savior, it was also his constant tormentor, but he could not exist without it.

I met Jerome Robbins in the middle of his life, when he was forty-eight and I was twenty-four. The struggle to create was always at the forefront of his mind. He was the only person I have ever known who was never at rest: he was always either thinking about his work or moving on to the next work or looking for new challenges. Over the many years of our friendship, the one constant of our discussions was the struggle to do good work.

I remember calling him once when I was working as a screenwriter in Los Angeles in the 1980s. I was going through a particularly arduous period of endless rewrites and battles with the producers over a script, trying to get it "right," and I was probably whining a bit on the phone that day. Jerry—if you knew him at all well, that's what you called him—listened patiently at first and then laughed and said, "That's why they call it work, Chris. If it was easy, then anyone could do it."

Robbins' lifelong flow of artistic energy began very early. From age three, he studied piano and violin and composed music. He wrote poetry, drew, painted, took photographs and apprenticed with a marionette puppet theater. He was good at all these activities and could have excelled in any one of them as an adult. He only began dancing in his late teens, but he trained with the focus and energy he would apply to everything he did for the rest of his life. By age twenty-three, Jerry was a featured soloist with Ballet Theatre, and at twenty-five in 1944, he was an overnight star and international name with a breakthrough ballet, *Fancy Free.*

It's hard to imagine seeing a career like his again. In musical theater, Robbins directed and choreographed a string of hits that includes the extraordinary and acclaimed *West Side Story* and *Fiddler on the Roof.* In the world of ballet, he choreographed nearly seventy original pieces, many of which became instant classics and comprise a significant part of the American Ballet Theatre and New York City Ballet repertoires and are performed by dance companies around the globe.

Unlike most of his contemporaries, Robbins did not make an exact distinction between theater dance and ballet dance. Interviewers were always trying to pin him down: Now you've left the theater, now you've left ballet... "No, no, I just work," he would say. It wasn't either/or, or whether he liked one form better than the other; for him, each project fed and informed the other. He began in dance, and dance remained his focus.

When Robbins joined Ballet Theatre as a dancer in the late 1930s, it was dominated by a Euro-Russian sensibility. To the ballet world, he brought "American" dancing and American "folk" music such as the blues and jazz rhythms from the street. He changed the contemporary dance vocabulary indelibly with his unique combination of clean and lyric classicism and the gestures and dances of everyday life. To musical theater, he brought a "populist" American authenticity and a masculine energy and athleticism that energized and forever elevated the standards of this art form. All his work was characterized by brilliant inventiveness and fierce energy, frequently spiced with the deliciously comic.

Try to think of another artist in the twentieth century that was simultaneously successful in both the "serious" ballet and the "commercial" theater on the highest level for as long a period. Today the worlds of serious art and commercial entertainment have spun out of orbit with each other and are so vast, so fragmented and specialized, that it could be Jerome Robbins will be remembered as the last to succeed in this way.

Some artists seem to leap out and define their age. Robbins' appetite for creative expression and the unique needs of the period he worked in meshed to forever alter the forms of musical theater and ballet. As he said himself, "Someone had to do it."

How to explain the unique combustion that caused his never-ending drive to create? Is it possible to decode the secret behind his genius? It doesn't do justice to his achievement to look for an answer in a purely psychological or determinist theory. Was it his early exposure to art through his mother? His need to live up to her perfectionism? His need to prove himself to his father and override his ridicule? His *other*ness within his own family? His sensitivity about being Jewish and an "outsider" in America? No one factor or combination of factors can fully account for Robbins' unrelenting creativity, his will, his ferocious energy and his extraordinary focus.

But there is no question that his experiences as a boy growing up in a large clan of Russian-Polish-Jewish immigrants in Weehawken, New Jersey, shaped him profoundly and provided many of the underlying themes for his art: the tension of living in an Old World atmosphere versus the desire to live and succeed as an American; the tension of holding on to the traditions of his ancestors versus embracing the modern world; the tension between men and women and the difficulties of connecting. The romantic triangle, in particular, would show up again and again in his work. All these issues became dominant themes in his creative work and life.

Here is the conundrum that continuously shaped Jerome Robbins' life: can you be an artist creating at the level, intensity and pace that he did, and also surrender in the way that is necessary to form loving partnerships?

When I first met Robbins in 1965, he had already been famous for half his life—as many years as I had lived. He had recently directed *Fiddler on the Roof,* for which he won his third and fourth Tony awards. Jerry was renting a house in the Hamptons on Long Island for the summer, as he had for several years. He had a strong affinity for the ocean. I was there on vacation from my job as a play reader for Broadway producer Kermit Bloomgarden. Friends took me one evening to a small dinner party in a converted barn in Water Mill.

From the instant I sat down at the table, Robbins' eyes lit up and he continued to stare and smile at me throughout the evening. I was more than just flattered—and yes, terrified—by his interest; I felt an instant, surprising connection with this man who seemed so apart from me and even the others at the table. Years later, his friend Aidan Mooney told me that upon asking Jerry how the two of us had gotten together, Jerry snapped his fingers like a dancer in *West Side Story* and said that we just instantly "clicked."

Being together was hardly a smooth ride, but we had more in common than might at first appeared. The idea of being "self-invented" in America was common to us both. He had been born into the thick of Russian-Jewish émigrés. I was two generations removed from Eastern Europe, but I could be plunged back into the Old World in an instant when visiting my Polish grandmother in Jersey City, New Jersey.

Following *Fiddler on the Roof,* Robbins was in a transition period in his working life. He had been working almost exclusively in the commercial theater since the late 1950s. Now he decided to take a break from it and was in the process of forming the American Theatre Lab to create an atmosphere in which to experiment with new theater forms. It was also a transition time in his personal life. He'd had serious relationships with both men and women, but a family life was something he longed for very much. When I met him in 1965, he felt time was running out if he was ever to marry and have children.

We shared a romantic summer in the Hamptons, and then got together in a serious way two years later. The winter of 1967, we began spending almost every weekend in a house Jerry rented in Sneden's Landing, New York. We became close friends with Dan and Ann Stern, a couple who lived next door, and years later, we would all look back on that time as a bubble of enchantment, with many pleasurable evenings spent cooking dinners for each other and sometimes night-skiing at a small slope nearby.

Jerry and I traveled together to Stockholm, London, Rome, Leningrad, Israel. After the trip to Israel, I moved into his house on 81st Street in New York City. In the spring of 1969, he choreographed *Dances at a Gathering* and we went to the premiere together.

Yet we could not sustain it. By the fall of that same year, I decided to move out. The reasons for parting at that time were many—some obvious, some not. The most pressing factor for me was that I knew I would never be strong enough to maintain an identity in his powerful force field. I felt I would not be able to forge a creative life of my own, something I very much wanted.

Perhaps because we were both then freed from—among many obstacles—our mutual idealization and expectations of marriage, tensions eased and our friendship flourished. We saw each other for dinner, the movies, and I went with him often to ballet events. Even later after I married and moved to California, Jerry and I remained close. I went to New York frequently for work and would stay at his house in the city. Most summers, I'd visit him in Long Island for a week or so. There were stretches of time when we were out of contact, but then we could always pick up immediately without a skipped beat.

For sixty years, Robbins' working life was concentrated over twenty-five square blocks of Manhattan, principally in the West Fifties. As a teenager, he took the ferry from Weehawken to Manhattan for dance class. His primary ballet teacher, Ella Daganova, had a studio on West 56th Street, and Robbins' first apartment when he began performing with Ballet Theatre was at 55th Street and Sixth Avenue. He and his fellow dancers would hang out at the Horn & Hardart automat on 57th Street, trading jokes and information about jobs. Robbins met his most significant collaborator, Leonard Bernstein, at Carnegie Hall on West 57th Street. Ballet Theatre and New York City Ballet were both in the West Fifties as well, and the Theater District nearby housed Robbins' many successes on stage.

Those who only know of the later Jerome Robbins—erect, handsome, bearded, guarded—would probably be surprised to hear of early descriptions of him that emphasize how high spirited and full of fun he was. Donald Saddler, a friend and fellow dancer from Ballet Theatre days, said that Jerry was always laughing, always playing jokes. Tanaquil Le Clercq, who remained a lifelong friend, called him a "genius gypsy" with "a wicked sense of humor" and told me that he was the best companion and always full of mischief. Robbins was an excellent dancer and completely fearless when performing. As Hermes in *Helen of Troy,* his first major star role for Ballet Theatre, he is remembered for upstaging the ballerinas with his inventive comic turns.

As years passed, the weight of life experience set in and the boyish exuberance was greatly tempered, but it never left altogether. Among friends with whom he felt relaxed, Jerry always loved a good laugh. I remember one day he called me in California to tell me the following story: he had called his answering service over the weekend for his messages. The operator relayed to him that a Mr. Schnickoff had called. Jerry insisted he didn't know a Mr. Schnickoff. The operator impatiently whined: "Schnickoff, Schnickoff ... Barry Schnickoff." Jerry laughed and laughed over that story. Told it to everyone he could. Particularly Baryshnikov.

Robbins took full advantage of the recognition and acclaim he achieved with his first ballet *Fancy Free* in 1944. He began working on several fronts at the same time: choreographing *On The Town* on Broadway (which was based on *Fancy Free*) and a succession of Broadway musicals in the years after, as well as making new ballets for Ballet Theatre and then New York City Ballet. Meanwhile, he continued to perform lead roles in his own and other ballets. Along the way, he even conceived and choreographed a musical, *Look, Ma, I'm Dancin'!,* which was a send-up of his experiences at Ballet Theatre. Here he was, still under thirty, with an autobiography on Broadway. The lead character was drawn with surprising ironic detachment as a Young Man In A Big Hurry To Succeed.

And that he certainly was. But wanting to succeed did not mean stinting on effort or excellence. Even those works Robbins would later consider "light-hearted" Broadway fare he approached with a seriousness of purpose, and his strong work habits set in early. He applied in equal measure: energy, research, preparation, effort, focus and perfectionism.

Harold Prince, who produced both *West Side Story* and *Fiddler on the Roof,* said Robbins was "one of the most prepared people" he ever worked with. And though Robbins was indeed a perfectionist, that didn't mean formal rigidity or lack of openness or a resistance to suggestion. He loved what he called "mistakes" or "accidents," as he was constantly on the lookout for something that would bring visual excitement and energy to the moment. Once, he saw dancer Nora Kaye coming out of a shower after rehearsal with her hair slicked back, and he used the look for her part in *The Cage.* So many of Robbins' ballets demonstrate his unique ability to take everyday objects and turn them into surprising props for his dances: umbrellas, chairs, balloons, streamers, hats, even trains.

Over time, the pressure of maintaining his exacting standards became more difficult. The stakes—both artistic and financial—got higher and higher. Robbins became known as a grueling taskmaster and demanding perfectionist. In his daily life, when he couldn't turn off his need to be in control, his perfectionism turned into a form of compulsiveness and fussiness. His mood could turn dark and fiercely angry, which was a double-edged sword: it fueled his creativity and drive to prove himself, but it could also push away those closest to him.

In order to get what he envisioned in his mind on the stage, Robbins could be cruel, he could bully, he could be insensitive to another's fatigue or physical pain. But the person he drove hardest was himself. He admired Balanchine for his detached and calm approach to choreography, but that was not Robbins' way. He was wired differently and needed to access his feelings and emotions more directly as he felt his way through a work. Although infinitely more stressful in the short term, the fruits of his approach appear everywhere in the work, which is steeped in emotion and dramatic intensity.

Those who worked with Robbins describe almost to the word a certain look he would get—when the thunderclouds rolled in and his eyes went blackblack. It was best then to get out of the way, not take it personally and wait until the sun came out again. Because when the light did shine again, he would fire up his collaborators and everyone else around him with an exuberant charge of inspiration. Some who worked with him remember only the tears, but those who were up to the challenge were left with a deep gratitude, knowing that being tempered with his fire forced them to rise to their full potential.

In his early career, Robbins thrived on collaboration. He loved sharing ideas, the joint problem solving, the fixing and refixing. His most powerful and defining collaboration was with Leonard Bernstein. They were the same age and complementary in temperament—Bernstein the more Dionysian, Robbins the more Apollonian—and together they became famous at age twenty-five for *Fancy Free.* Their collaboration would reach a pinnacle of creative power in *West Side Story.*

Following this great success, though, neither would ever find another collaborator who energized and complemented the other in the same way. When they did try to work together in the later years, they were no longer "Lenny" and "Jerry" but now Leonard Bernstein and Jerome Robbins. The need to create important works together left them both dissatisfied with the results. Although they tried several times, they never could duplicate the perfect fits of *Fancy Free* and *West Side Story.*

Robbins was grateful for his mentors and always credited them. The first person who encouraged him as a dancer was Gluck-Sandor, who ran a pioneering modern dance troupe in the 1930s. Sandor was the first to give Robbins a sense of what it meant to be an artist—particularly the possibilities for joy in it—and how one went about working at a craft. Later, the legendary theater director George Abbott—who, when Robbins met him, was already a great presence on Broadway—became an important mentor and collaborator. They went on to do six shows together, two of which they co-directed. Mr. Abbott, as he was always called, was known to sign notes to Jerry with "Your Assistant, Abbott." The other important George in Robbins' life, George Balanchine, remained his most important and influential artistic guide for forty years. Jerry fondly referred to them as Mr. A and Mr. B.

In the Broadway theater, particularly with his contemporaries, Robbins fought hard for position and credit. When he began working as a choreographer, this artistic category was notoriously underpaid, under-credited and undervalued, and he responded tenaciously to correct injustices. He knew the value of his own work and also knew that in the commercial theater how much he was paid created power in itself. He wasn't afraid to use his power, paving the way for choreographers who followed him. Robbins negotiated to own the rights to his choreography for *High Button Shoes,* something unheard of at the time. He was a good businessman—not that common a trait among creative people—paying close attention to his contracts and fighting hard for billing. He is particularly famous among Broadway-ites for inventing the box around his name in the credits. Needless to say, Robbins stirred jealousy and he created enemies.

Yet in an atmosphere where competition wasn't necessary, Robbins could exist peacefully and collegially, without the need for any trappings of power. At New York City Ballet, he shared a small office-*cum*-locker room with George Balanchine for over forty years. He happily accepted the title of Associate Ballet Master. Some of his ballets paid only a pittance in performance royalties. He claims to have fought only once with Balanchine in all the years they worked together. Although their relationship necessarily rearranged itself with time, the feeling of mutual respect between them never left.

Those who view success through the glass of envy expect success to always contain success. Jerry once told me that his family idealized his life, expecting that he ate a successful breakfast, then went on to a successful lunch and so on, not understanding that his life was difficult and could contain deep pain.

I was witness to many of his disappointments, both personal and professional. In my naiveté, I was surprised to discover over the course of time that Robbins' friendships were no less fragile than my own: friends could wound you, treat you carelessly or simply disappear from your life, and being famous did not protect you from these experiences. When I was helping Jerry research a film project on the legendary dancer Vaslav Nijinsky, I remember being stunned when the producer abruptly decided to drop him as director.

Reading through early clippings of his career, I discovered so many announcements of film projects that never happened. Robbins' success in ballet and on Broadway brought attention from the movie studios, but Hollywood would remain for him a continuing siren call, ever elusive, always full of disappointment.

His biggest disappointment in Hollywood came after one of his greatest artistic successes—*West Side Story.* Hired to co-direct the film version with Robert Wise, Robbins conceived the spectacular opening aerial dance shots and major dance numbers, notably "Cool," which unarguably give the film its power and originality. Then he was fired by the producers, and his assistants choreographed the remaining dance numbers. Whatever the whole truth behind this occurrence, Robbins accepted the Academy Award for Best Director in 1961, along with an

Honorary Academy Award for his "brilliant achievements" in choreo-graphy, but his feelings ran so high and deep on the subject that from then on he refused to set foot in the state of California, as if the whole state were to blame. He made an exception when he flew in to see dancer Nora Kaye before she died in 1987. They had known each other since the early days at Ballet Theatre, had once been engaged and remained great friends. In 1991, he went to California one last time, for the Los Angeles opening of *Jerome Robbins' Broadway.*

To have only known Jerome Robbins in a working environment would give you little clue to the complexity of the man in his private life. He had perhaps an innate sense of privacy, an inherited wariness of the "other" from his Jewish family. Trusting others did not come easily. As he grew older, the austere and guarded Jerome Robbins came more and more to dominate the friendly and approachable Jerry. All his life, he struggled to manage his volatile emotions, and the hard shell he presented to the world covered vulnerabilities and sensitivities very close to the surface and too easily activated. Until he committed himself fully to something, he could be famously indecisive. Many producers went gray waiting for him to commit to a show. When a trip loomed—whether for work or pleasure—he obsessed for days before, always ready to cancel at the last moment—and often he did.

Despite his boldness as a creator, he was surprisingly shy in social situations. Small talk did not come easily, and I would tease him that if I truly wanted to torture him, I would take him to a cocktail party where he knew no one. But once his outer shell of mistrust was cracked and you were fortunate enough to enter into his private realm, he could be the most amazing friend. The level of concern he gave to those he cared about was deep and boundless. He provided generous support to his family from the time he had money of his own to the end of his life. When his housekeeper was hospitalized for breast cancer surgery, he arrived at her bedside every day at 7:00 AM with orange juice he had squeezed himself. When his close friend and former lover Jesse Gerstein was dying of AIDs, Jerry took him into his house, paid all the hospital and twenty-four-hour nursing bills, and personally cared for him to the end. In my own case, when I was seriously ill over several years in the early 1990s, he was my most constant and caring friend. He never slipped in his attention to me, despite the tediousness of the long illness, and when I needed it, he paid for a live-in nurse.

Robbins was also a generous mentor and supporter of other artists, assisting many choreographers, including Bob Fosse and Eliot Feld, in their careers. In addition to financial support through his nonprofit dance foundation, he would embrace artists he admired with the full force of his enthusiasm. He discovered the theater artist Robert Wilson at the beginning of his career and gave him substantial financial support over twenty years, but his most valuable support was through championing Wilson's work. As critical and exacting as Robbins could be, when he admired something, he admired it wholly. When he was enchanted by a dancer's performance, he loved it with a childlike wonder and appreciation.

Though Robbins protected himself personally, he liked to stay open to the new, resisting a life that would be too formal or "frozen in ice," a phrase he used. For the sake of staying fresh, he went to avant garde and experimental performances in the lofts and alternative spaces in New York City. He liked to stay close to the ground, so to speak, resisting the overly posh or chic. He made friends in widely disparate circles—always finding rare qualities in the people he encountered in his daily life.

Despite Robbins' wealth, he remained simple in his tastes. I found him remarkably lacking in vanity about both his clothes and his body. He would buy high-quality clothes for public occasions, but his typical daily outfit was jeans and the light cotton mandarin-collared shirts he favored. After years of training and performing as a dancer, he chose to get most of his exercise from his work in rehearsal, and he did not obsess about his fitness or physique.

Robbins' houses were comfortable, but not opulent or "done," and his art collection was more personal and eclectic than expensive. He had a Depression-era kid's resistance to "unnecessary spending." He agonized for weeks over an extra five thousand dollars for the oceanfront beach cottage in Bridgehampton, New York, that he bought in 1982.

Cars were another case in point. When I first met Jerry, he was driving a black Karmann Ghia convertible. It was a cute and zippy car, but hardly a rich man's car. He enjoyed driving it so much that he had a difficult time parting with it. When I lived with him, he'd had the car for at least fifteen years, and it was with the mechanic more often than on the road. Jerry kept talking about getting a new car…but…always finding a reason to put it off. Finally I said, "Come on, we're going to the Mercedes dealer and we're going to buy a new car today." I forget who picked Mercedes—but the idea was a good, solid car.

At the dealership, he pulled back from the large burgher models. He could not imagine himself driving one of those. We settled on a Mercedes 280 SL coupe in a powder blue color. It was not exactly ideal, but it was the only one on the floor. I nudged him to write a check then and there, and we drove off in the car. This was the last car Robbins owned. He drove it for thirty years, then passed it on to friends in his will. And the powder blue Mercedes is still on the road today.

A dark shadow crept over Robbins' dazzling aura of success when he testified in 1953 before the House Un-American Activities Committee (HUAC). Having been subjected to intense pressure and threatened with exposure relating to his sexual life for two years, he was persuaded by his lawyer to testify about his membership in the Communist party in his late twenties and to give names of others that attended meetings with him.

He never spoke publicly about his testimony after appearing before the committee. He never tried to justify his actions. The atmosphere around Robbins in the Broadway theater world became highly toxic as many of his contemporaries branded him an informer and became openly hostile. He felt it would be futile to attempt to explain himself under those circumstances.

But remarkably, the scalding experience with HUAC in 1953 did not stop Robbins from working. His gloriously lyrical ballet, *Afternoon of a Faun,* debuted the week after his appearance before the committee, presenting a stark contrast to the committee's ugly business. Tanaquil Le Clercq remembers that he choreographed it very quickly and surely on her, with great energy and focus. In fact, a case can be made that the experience with HUAC ignited an even greater need within Robbins to prove himself. In the years that followed, he produced works of increasing stature—*West Side Story* in 1957 and *Fiddler on the Roof* in '64, *Dances at a Gathering* (1969), *The Goldberg Variations* (1971) and the many ballets he created during his long and fruitful years at New York City Ballet.

One weekend in Sneden's Landing, he decided to discuss with me what had happened. I thought I was being sympathetic by saying it was okay, he didn't need to, but he really wanted me to hear him out and my response frustrated him. I remember he told me how difficult it was to sort out all the conflicting advice and information he received and how impossible it was to trust anyone, including his own lawyer. He said his lawyer, who represented a number of clients in similar situations, counseled them all to cooperate with the committee, insisting that it was *pro forma* to give names of other people attending the meetings and that in any case the committee already knew their names.

I remember he also told me how his work had been his way to establish an identity, that he couldn't separate himself from his work. He told me he had had the irrational fear that if he did not comply, he would go straight back to the Weehawken world he had fought so hard to escape.

Years later he tried to deal with all his bottled-up emotions and make sense of the experience in what came to be called *Poppa Piece,* an autobiographical, theatrical dance-drama that he worked on, sometimes as a form of therapy, for over twenty-five years. In 1991, Robbins finally felt able to take a stab at staging the piece and began a workshop production of *Poppa Piece* at Lincoln Center. The scenes representing his early life were staged quickly, but I remember those who worked with him saying that as much as Jerry tried to stage the scenes of his trial testimony—emotionally searing on paper—he could not completely unravel all the multiple strands of meaning and emotions for himself. Ultimately, he withdrew the production.

In 1972 when he was fifty-two, Robbins began keeping a journal. The Japanese rice paper notebooks he used were 11 1/2 by 3 1/2 inches in size and covered in distinctive woodblock prints. The notebooks opened accordion style, so that you could write across two pages, then turn them over and write on the back side. In all, Robbins produced twenty-three journals—an extraordinary document of his inner and outer life until 1984. He sometimes wrote daily or sometimes just when traveling. He wrote and drew with pencil, pen or watercolors. He made collages, using mementos of his travels or any artifact evocative of his experiences at the time.

Frequently brutally candid, the journals record a period in his life when he was questioning everything, detailing personal losses (but also personal pleasures), venting fears about being able to continue his work. These journals are a closely observed journey of his soul during that period. In his will, Robbins gave instructions that the personal writings in these journals not be shown to the public until fifteen years after his death. I am grateful to the Robbins Estate for allowing me to include fourteen of the journal pages—including collages he made when traveling, drawings, a monthly calendar and writings relating specifically to the work. No existing material relating to Robbins' life— and there are mountains of it as he kept everything!—gives greater insight into the intensely active artistic spirit of the man than these journal pages.

After the 1970s, Robbins' collaborations ended for the most part. He concentrated instead on ballets, embarking on a more interior journey at this time of his life, creating works more abstract and less outwardly story-driven. He said he preferred the "simplicity" of choreographing on his own at New York City Ballet with dancers he felt were the best in the world.

In his very last years, he was beset with health problems that would have stopped most people dead in their tracks but did not stop him. If he had a bad cold, he could get cranky, but a serious operation engendered no self-pity. He simply got on with what had to be done to get well and go on living. He used much of his remaining store of energy for preserving his works. *Jerome Robbins' Broadway* celebrated his Broadway shows, and he spent a great deal of time attending to his ballet repertoire.

And he went to a lot of memorials. If you worked with as many people of acclaim and stature as he did, you had the bittersweet honor of speaking at their memorials. One day Robbins came into his office and dropped his phone book down on a desk in front of his staff. "Will somebody please take all the dead people out of this book?" he said.

I don't think it is a coincidence that the very last work Jerome Robbins mounted was a wedding, a restaging of *Les Noces,* first choreographed by him in 1965. He had struggled all his life to achieve some peaceful union of the warring parts within himself, and it seemed to me that at the end of his life he no longer resisted so fiercely the shape his life had taken.

He frequently expressed to me in his later years that he felt gratitude for having his work. Referring to a mutual friend whom he felt was living a barren life as old age approached, Jerry said that work gave purpose and shape to his own life, as well as welcome solace during rough personal passages. Work could disappoint him, it could exhaust him, it often deserted him, but at its best, it gave Jerry the deepest kind of pleasure—down to the core of his soul. In many ways, work had become his closest friend.

WHITE STAR LINE.

S.S. _____ '1924

Dear Daddy,

How are you?
We are in the middle of
the Ocean.
I am not sea-sick.
Every night we have
ice cream.

from Jerry

Jerome Robbins' journal, 1977. Robbins was
a 5-year-old with his mother on a ship bound
for Poland and a visit with relatives when
he wrote this letter to his father. He kept the
letter at his house on East 81st Street —
framed on the desk in his office. When he was
59, he created this collage, which includes a
photograph of himself in the lower right corner.

1

BEGINNINGS
THE MAKING OF AN ARTIST
1918–1939

"When I was a child, art seemed like a tunnel to me. At the end of that tunnel I could see light where the world opened up, waiting..."

He was born Jerome Rabinowitz, to Harry and Lena (née Rips) Rabinowitz on October 11, 1918 in New York City. Harry worked with his brothers in a family-owned delicatessen at 51 East 97th Street in Manhattan, and, along with other Jewish immigrants from Eastern Europe, the Rabinowitz family—Harry, Lena, Jerry and his sister Sonia—lived in the large building above, which still stands today.

When the delicatessen was sold in the 1920s, the family moved to Jersey City, New Jersey, home to Lena's parents, Ida and Aaron Rips, who were both active in Jewish affairs in the section of that city known as The Heights. Shortly after, the young family moved again to nearby Weehawken, and Harry and Lena went into the corset business with relatives. Lena was one of six sisters and one brother, and the combined Rabinowitz and Rips clans formed a large, tight-knit family.

The six Rips sisters were particularly close. Lena was the second oldest but was considered first among them, with a fierce intelligence and strong organizing skills. Jerry's sister Sonia described them to me as women who "together could rule the world." Lena was also a leader in her own household, as Harry Rabinowitz was seen as a man who deferred to his wife. But Harry had a lively sense of humor, whereas Lena apparently had little or none. Jerry's personality combined Lena's intellectual strengths with Harry's high spirits, yet the highly complex Rabinowitz family dynamics left a heavy imprint, and throughout his lifetime Jerry struggled to sort out all the painful psychological wounds.

Lena Rabinowitz actively encouraged her children's participation in the arts. Sonia, six years older than Jerry, was the dancer in the family—a prodigy who performed in recitals from the age of three and later toured as a "barefoot dancer" with a company run by Irma Duncan, a daughter of Isadora Duncan. Jerry studied piano and violin, inventing his own music compositions and playing the piano in concerts. He wrote poetry and stories, too, and painted and made puppets.

"The only world that was really exciting to me," he once said, "Was the world in which I could make believe that things were not the way they were." From a very early age, he had the desire to do something in the arts. He often practiced dancing with Sonia, and he danced in amateur shows at the summer camp Kittatinny, but the idea that a boy could become a dancer—or worse still, consider it a profession—was anathema to both parents, particularly the father, Harry.

As a young teenager, Jerry accompanied his sister Sonia on the ferry from Weehawken across the Hudson River to Manhattan, which seemed to them an island of endless

above left. At 51 East 97th Street, New York City.

below left. In front of 108 Booream Avenue, his parents' home in Jersey City, New Jersey.

right. Harry Rabinowitz holding his son, Jerome, with arm around daughter, Sonia, in front of family delicatessen at 51 East 97th Street in New York City.

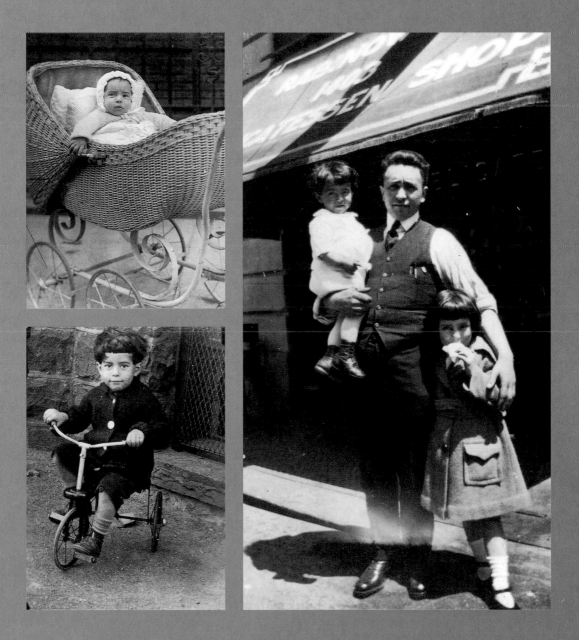

possibility, including, among so much else, Senia Gluck-Sandor and Felicia Sorel's pioneering school of modern dance, The Dance Center, where Sonia began performing in the early 1930s. Robbins occasionally took classes along with her, and it was Gluck-Sandor who persuaded the reluctant Rabinowitzes to let their son try dancing for at least a year.

"He had what you call a photographic memory," Gluck-Sandor said, spotting the young man's talent at once. "Once he saw something, he could do it backward. Before I would do a thing, he had it. He could anticipate what was to come. He was sensitive and he was musical. I spoke to his parents and said, 'Why not let the boy become a dancer? If he doesn't like it, OK. But it might be good for him.' He was kind of slender and frail then.... So they agreed and he stopped school and plunged into it."

"My parents were Russian-Jewish émigrés who felt it was necessary to give their children as much culture are possible. My sister [Sonia] got dance classes and we both got piano classes. And we were taken to museums and concerts as well.... So we always kept going to New York for the cultural aspects of life. And that turned my sister and me on in a way we liked."

Harry and Lena Rabinowitz with their two
children, Sonia and Jerome.

above. Rabinowitz family in Russia. Bearded patriarch is Robbins' grandfather, known as Notre Mayer.

right. Aaron Rips surrounded by his children (from left) Gertrude, Jean, Jake, Mary, Anna and Lena (Robbins' mother). Youngest daughter Francis is not present. Note the startling resemblance Jerome had as an adult to his maternal grandfather in this picture.

Jerome (front, with violin) in the music
and theory class of Effa Ellis Perfield, 36 East
36th Street, New York City. Robbins' mother
brought first Sonia and then Jerome to study
with Miss Perfield, who is said to have proudly
kept all of Robbins' early compositions,
beginning from age 3.

above. Sonia "barefoot dancing" a la Isadora
Duncan at Alyce Bentley's school, Studio 61 in
Carnegie Hall.

left. Sonia Rabinowitz, age 4, at a recital.

left. Jerome Robbins, in a performance of *Danse Macabre* at Camp Kittatinny in Dingman's Ferry, New Jersey, a summer camp owned by relatives, which the family frequented in the early 1930s. The camp had a small theater where Robbins danced and performed in several Gilbert and Sullivan musicals.

above. The Dramatic Club at Woodrow Wilson High School, Weehawken, New Jersey. Robbins graduated in 1935. In 1936, he attended New York University, studying chemistry, but with the Depression, the family business suffered a setback and Robbins dropped out his freshman year. Somehow, his family was able to scrape together enough money to pay for his classes at the Sandor-Sorel Dance Center.

> "I liked chemistry, writing, poetry and music.
> I even thought I wanted to be a puppeteer.
> I did **NOT** want to go into my father's [corset]
> business...."

The Comfort Corset Factory in Union
City, New Jersey, where Harry and Lena
Rabinowitz worked together.

"I started training quite late. I started taking ballet lessons when I was about 16-17. Before that I had watched my sister take classes, which were sort of Duncanish classes, and I would occasionally take them with her. Then she began working with Gluck-Sandor and Felicia Sorel, who had a modern dance company above a garage on 54th Street."

Camp Tamiment, PA. 1939 *SnaPPy*

Camp Tamiment, Pa. 1938 *"Snappy"*

728 14

40

"This was in the late '30s, up in Camp Tamiment
... a summer adult camp up in the Poconos.
They had a rather large entertainment staff,
especially for those times. It was run by Max
Liebman, who did *Your Show of Shows.* It
was my first paying job as a dancer. And there
I met Imogene Coca, Danny Kaye. I worked
with Anita Alvarez, who was one of Martha
Graham's major dancers at the time.... And it
was an extraordinary training field. We had to
do three different shows each week.... So
we got a chance to do just about anything we
wanted to do.... I first started doing solos
for myself. Then I did some duets, and then
I wanted to do something bigger."

Camp Tamiment in Bushkill, Pennsylvania.
The resort in the Pocono Mountains main-
tained a large entertainment staff, and
Robbins worked there over five summers,
creating his first choreography. His early work
was sometimes serious and political in
content, as in "Strange Fruit," choreographed
to Billie Holiday's haunting recording of Lewis
Allen's song about lynchings in America.

Senia Gluck-Sandor and Felicia Sorel
demonstrating their modern dance take on
the Charleston. At Gluck-Sandor's urging,
Robbins studied ballet—washing Venetian
blinds for teacher Ella Daganova in exchange
for three lessons a week. Daganova was an
American who danced with Pavlova (ballet
teachers in this period often took a Russian
name). Robbins also studied oriental dance
with Nimura, Spanish dancing with Helena
Veola and "interpretive" dance with his sister
and Alyce Bentley. The variety in Robbin's
training reflects the dance world in the 1930s,
and Robbins often said this may have been a
factor in his ease in crossing boundaries in
his later work.

"Gluck-Sandor said to me quite early in our
training, 'You better study ballet.' I said,
'Ballet, yech!' He said, 'No, no, no. You should
study it, because it's going to come back.
It's going to come back full force, and you
should know it. You should get that technique
in your body while you still can, while you're
still growing.'"

"Gluck-Sandor was unique because he could
see the positive side of anything that
would get in his way. If there were three poles
coming down from the ceiling in the studio,
he used them. If there was anything that could
be improvised, he used it. And he used it
very deeply."

BARBIZON-PLAZA

"The honors of the season belong to the Dance Center."
—MARY WATKINS, *Herald Tribune.*

THE DANCE CENTER

America's Only Ballet Company

Saturday Evening, December 10, 1932

PROGRAM

"TEMPO"

(Dance Marathon)

A NEW AMERICAN BALLET

Music by Herbert Kingsley—Decorations by Reginald Marsh—Choreographical Direction by Gluck-Sandor—Scenario by Robert M. Coates.

CAST

(In order of appearance)

Team 1	Sonya Robyns, Frank Pujol
Team 2	Tashamira, Jacques Cartier
Team 3	Felicia Sorel, Randolph Sawyer
Team 4	Blanche Schocket, Gregor Taksa
Team 5	Bunty Klein, Louis Rosen
Team 6	Eve Desca, Miss Etille
Team 7	Sybil Blanc, Irving Lansky
Sister Team	Gladys Shermer, Adele Kellogg
Team 8	Claire Lea, Richard Stuart
Scrubwoman	Mercedes Guthrie
Nurse	Hana Geiger
Hoofer	Gluck-Sandor

ACT 1—First hour.

ACT 2—One hundred and seventy-seventh hour.

ACT 3—Ten hundred and thirty-second hour.

At the Piano, FLORENCE KYTE

Gowns and Costumes for 1st Act.................T F. Brigance and Joro

BALLET REPERTOIRE OF THE DANCE CENTER

"Petrouchka" by Stravinsky	"El Amor Brujo" by de Falle
"Salome" by Richard Strauss	"The Prodigal Son" by Prokofieff

Productions Scheduled for 1932-1933

"Phobia" based on John Vassos' book and designs, music by A. Lehman Engel

"The Three Cornered Hat" by de Falle	"Les Sylphides" by Chopin
"Till Eulenspiegel" by Richard Strauss	"Afternoon of a Faun" by Debussy

EXECUTIVE STAFF FOR THE DANCE CENTER

Directors	Gluck-Sandor and Felicia Sorel
Manager	Grace Duncan Hooper
Technical Director	Frank Brownlow

Performances every Saturday evening, and other evenings to be announced.

above. Program from The Sandor-Sorel Dance Center performance at the Barbizon-Plaza Hotel on December 10, 1932. Robbins' sister Sonia is listed on the program as "Sonya Robyns." Two artist cousins also used the name Robyns when exhibiting their work, and Jerry spelled his name this way while he was at Camp Tamiment.

right. In its 1934-1935 season, The Dance Center called its company, The American Ballet, though it was a modern dance company. The ambitious repertory consisted of 30 pieces, remarkable for the period.

"Gluck-Sandor...had a passion about the performance itself. I don't know how much of it was...influenced by his work that he was doing with the Group Theater at the time, which had just begun.... We worked in the 'center of concentration' so that no one could bother us [by] being very close to us, because the audience sat as close as any two people in a room. It was a very, very tiny place.

"I was inspired by everything he did."

Permanent Theater Ass'n, Inc.

Announces the 1934-35 Season
of
AMERICAN BALLET

Director   Artistic-Director-Choreographer
WILLIAM FLINN   GLUCK-SANDOR

THE AMERICAN BALLET is an outgrowth of the Dance Center and is offering for the 1934-5 Season a number of striking presentations from its repertory of thirty ballets.

A distinctive list of well known ballets will be given, such as Stravinsky's "Petrouchka" and the "Love Sorceress" by De Falla. Also a number of exciting modern works, startling in their dynamic forcefulness. The "Prodigal Son," "Masks and Hands", and others as important.

Repertory of Ballets

Petrouchka	Dream Phobias	Picassoesque
Salome	Fire Ritual	Afternoon of a Faun
The Prodigal Son	Tempo (Dance Marathon)	Mask and Hands
The Love Sorceress	Lillies of the Field	(feature of the late Vanities)

The ballets, will be supplemented with the repertory of divertissements, including a group of authentic American Negro Blues.

Pagannini	Magdalene	Pride
New Yorker	Renunciation	Millers Dance
Night	Ascension	(choreography Escudero)
Sea Gull	Lust	Animalia
Dark Angel	Vanity	Bedouine
Seven Deadly Sins	Covetousness	Song of the Damned
Angel		
Duo-Creations:		

"Lida and the Swan" by Wilens. "The Penthouse" with sound arrangements. "Narcissus and Echo" by Debussy. "Kabbala" with Authentic Folk Song. "Geometric and Metronome" and "Puppet Sarcasms", Music by Prokofieff.

"Gluck-Sandor gave me…a chance to dance in *El Amor Brujo*…. Many years later, I was talking to my father and I said, 'Pop, what did you think of my dancing?' He said, 'Ah, I knew you'd be all right.' I said, 'How did you know that?' He said, 'Once you were dancing that Spanish dance…and [critic] John Martin was there. I went up and spoke to John Martin.' I said, 'What! You spoke to John Martin?' 'Yes…I said to him, "What do you think of that boy who just did that dance?" He said, "Oh, I think he's very good." So I knew you'd be all right.'"

Jerome Robbins appeared in Gluck-Sandor's
El Amor Brujo, with music by Manuel De Falle,
1933. This story of a possession resembles
the underlying story of *Dybbuk*, which Robbins
discussed with Leonard Bernstein as a
possible subject for collaboration as early
as 1949.

"Because I looked four years younger than I actually was, I was called in to play the part of the brothers' father as a child [in *The Brothers Ashkenazi*]. I didn't really know Yiddish—my parents only used the language when they didn't want me to understand something. But all I had to say was, 'yuh, Tata,' meaning 'yes, Father.' The whole thing was a wonderful experience for me, though. Those actors—this was a Maurice Schwartz show—were fantastic. When we stopped general rehearsals and went into dress rehearsal, the art of makeup was so extraordinary that I literally didn't recognize anyone.

"It was an enormously long show, I remember. I only had to appear in the first and third scenes in Act I, and that left me time to take a walk in the park, have lunch, go to the zoo, and still come back in plenty of time to make the opening of the second act. Oh yeah, we also had a strike. The actors played every night of the week and twice on Saturdays and Sundays, for which we got $10. So we struck, and they made it $15."

Gluck-Sandor provided choreography for
plays at the Yiddish Art Theatre. A member
of the dance company, Robbins was cast
in a speaking role in the production of *The
Brothers Ashkenazi* in 1937. It's hard not to
think that memories of this scene from the
play provided inspiration for Robbins' staging
of the scene of Tevye and Golde in bed in
Fiddler on the Roof.

above. Albert Einstein visiting backstage at the Yiddish Art Theatre, following a performance of *The Brothers Ashkenazi.* Also present are Mayor Fiorello LaGuardia, Maurice Schwartz, producer, and members of the cast, including a young and proud Jerome Robbins.

above right. A poster for *The Brothers Ashkenazi.* The program is the earliest record of Robbin's use of "Jerome Robbins" as his stage name.

"It was a rough period. My parents were footing a lot of my bills because I wasn't making enough money.... But as soon as I began to earn my own living, the battle was over. Then I learned that I had really been fighting to break away from the family."

2

THE PATH TO FANCY FREE
1940–1944

"There was...in the late 1930s...very little dance.
No ballet companies, no heavy classes, everyone grabbing at whatever was being offered—
quick performances, quick little guarantees....
There were few musicals. We all worked on
Broadway until Ballet Theatre decided to make
a company—and then how we all flew to it.
Sad days and happy days. We were a small
group and we all knew each other and kept
our ears open to get any chance at a job."

Jerome Robbins kneeling at the feet of Tamara
Toumanova, in a production of *Stars in Your
Eyes* at the Majestic Theatre, 1939.

Ballet Theatre began its first season in January of 1940, and Robbins auditioned shortly afterwards in May. He was very proud to be asked to join the company, recalling later that out of hundreds who auditioned only fourteen dancers were chosen.

Ballet Theatre proved to be an excellent training ground and, in typical fashion, Robbins absorbed its lessons quickly. As a dancer, he distinguished himself as having unique comic gifts on stage. Agnes de Mille, who was working with Ballet Theatre at the time, remembered that Robbins was well-known among the dancers as the boy who could count like a whiz. She was looking for someone to portray the Youth for her ballet *Three Virgins and a Devil,* and none of the other dancers could do the "intricate jazzy kind of counting out of the music." Robbins learned what she had to teach him in "twelve and a half minutes," and then "he stopped the show."

The majority of ballets performed at Ballet Theatre were hardly breaking new ground in the new dancer's eyes, and Robbins began to think about choreographing on his own. He submitted a number of scenarios for ambitious ballets with "casts of thousands," as he joked later. One day, Ballet Theatre canceled a project, an opening appeared in the schedule, and Robbins was told that if he could come up with a short one-act ballet, the company would put it on.

He had long had the simmering idea that if the Russians used their folk music and lore for ballets, why shouldn't Americans use American music and themes? Why not add movement that is natural and contemporary to the traditional dance vocabulary and use American social dances? Robbins' friend Mary Hunter, who ran the American Actors Company, suggested he base a ballet on *The Fleet's In*, a painting by Paul Cadmus. While Robbins was taken with the images of soldiers on leave in wartime, he felt the painting's tone was "too raunchy." He began to work with the basic theme, and the end result differed widely from its inspiration. Because he had to sell a composer on his idea, Robbins wrote an extremely detailed scenario for what became his first major ballet, *Fancy Free.*

"I first met George Balanchine when he selected me for a show called *Great Lady.* I was very proud to have been picked for it because most of the people were from the School of American Ballet, which I wasn't attending at the time."

Jerome Robbins "swashbuckling" in *Great Lady*, 1938, a musical choreographed by George Balanchine, whom Robbins met for the first time. Balanchine later asked Robbins to understudy Jose Limon in *Keep Off the Grass*.

Stars in Your Eyes, Majestic Theatre, 1939.
Robbins is on far left.

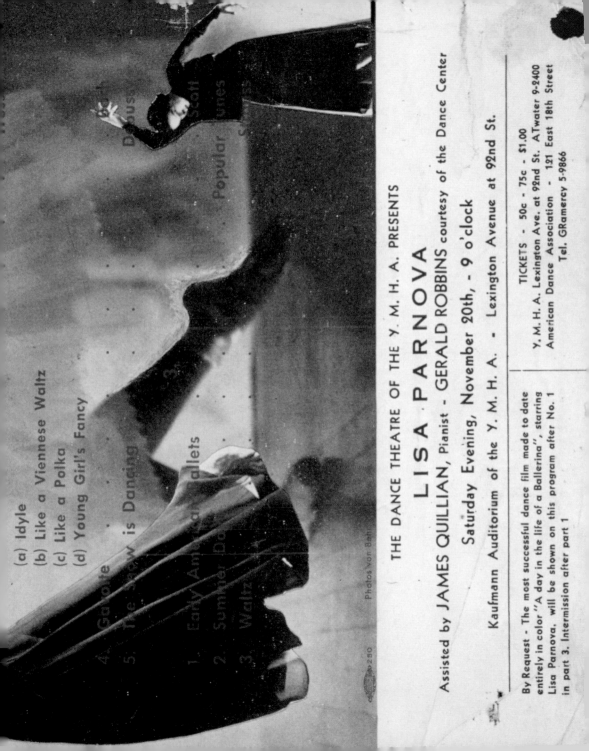

(a) Idyle
(b) Like a Viennese Waltz
(c) Like a Polka
(d) Young Girl's Fancy

5. The Snow is Dancing

... Gavotte

Popular Tunes

Debussy

Scott

Strauss

Early American Ballets

1. Early American Ballets
2. Summer Da...
3. Waltz
4. ...

Photos von Behl...

280

THE DANCE THEATRE OF THE Y. M. H. A. PRESENTS

LISA PARNOVA

Assisted by JAMES QUILLIAN, Pianist - GERALD ROBBINS courtesy of the Dance Center

Saturday Evening, November 20th, - 9 o'clock

Kaufmann Auditorium of the Y. M. H. A. - Lexington Avenue at 92nd St.

TICKETS - 50c - 75c - $1.00

Y. M. H. A. Lexington Ave. at 92nd St. ATwater 9-2400
American Dance Association - 121 East 18th Street
Tel. GRamercy 5-9866

By Request - The most successful dance film made to date entirely in color "A day in the life of a Ballerina", starring Lisa Parnova, will be shown on this program after No. 1 in part 3. Intermission after part 1

"... for a guy who's supposedly had as much success as I've had, almost everything I've tried for the first time was a flop.... The first time I danced in New York as a ballet dancer [was] as a partner for... Lisa Parnova, and the review said my partnering 'hindered more than helped.' And the first show I directed [*That's the Ticket*] closed out of town. People don't know those things—they tend to just see the scores and not the misses."

This was the first review Robbins (listed here as "Gerald Robbins") received as a dancer. It was not a good one.

Despite many initial rejections from composers he approached, Robbins didn't waver in his conviction about the worth of *Fancy Free* and stayed focused on his goal. With the practicality and strength of purpose he demonstrated throughout his career, he recognized that he was still an unknown and just had to keep looking. Finally he found the composer Leonard Bernstein, who at age 25 was already Assistant Conductor of the New York Philharmonic and had just finished writing his first symphony, *Jeremiah.*

An acute observer of the people and places around him, Robbins absorbed imagery from everyday life and used it in his dances. Ballet Theatre performed near 42nd Street, and Robbins' noticed that, among the tourists, sailors on leave usually went out in threes. He incorporated this pattern into his ballet. Janet Reed, one of the original company members of *Fancy Free* who was touring with Robbins while he was developing the ballet, remembers Robbins looking out of a train window and seeing an interesting formation of planes. He used this image, too, in *Fancy Free.*

Robbins' rehearsed the cast of his new ballet everywhere and anywhere—in hotel lobbies and hallways and ballrooms, in theater basements and momentarily empty stages—any space he could find while on tour. Already he displayed an intense working style, and he kept his head down despite difficult circumstances. When he looked up at the curtain call on the opening night of *Fancy Free,* April 18, 1944, he was famous.

Here is what John Martin, the influential dance critic of the *New York Times,* wrote about the ballet:

"To come right to the point without any ifs, ands, and buts, Jerome Robbins' *Fancy Free,* which the Ballet Theatre presented in its world premiere last night at the Metropolitan Opera House, is a smash hit. This [is] young Robbins' first go at choreography, and the only thing he has to worry about in that direction is how in the world he is going to make his second one any better. He has managed to get into this light-hearted little piece of American genre the same quality of humor which has always characterized his personal dancing, the same excellent actor's sense of the theatre, and some first-rate invention to boot."

"Better buy your tickets in advance. It is going to be one of those things."

"[When I joined Ballet Theatre in 1940], I thought how beautiful to be able to dance something different every night as opposed to the life I was leading on Broadway. First, there was the agonizing experience of auditioning for a show. Then, if it was a hit, you were stuck with it.

"At Ballet Theatre, I got the opportunity to work for all the choreographers. The best education you could have. I had the privilege of working with Fokine, Massine, Tudor, Nijinska, Lichine, Balanchine, Loring and de Mille—and that's just for starters."

Dark Elegies, choreographed by Antony Tudor for Ballet Theatre. Seeing this ballet as a spectator in 1939 is what made Robbins want to join the company. Robbins, standing on right, began performing this masterwork of Tudor's in 1942.

Nº 785

Form B-2
January 1, 1940

AMERICAN GUILD OF MUSICAL ARTISTS Inc.

(BRANCH OF ASSOCIATED ACTORS AND ARTISTES OF AMERICA)

AFFILIATED WITH AMERICAN FEDERATION OF LABOR

545 FIFTH AVENUE · NEW YORK

TELEPHONE
VANDERBILT 6-6340

STANDARD CONTRACT FOR EMPLOYMENT

BY THE WEEK

FOR USE FOR EMPLOYMENT IN OPERA, CONCERT, RECITAL, BALLET AND DANCE, CHORUS AND CHOIR, AND FOR OTHER TYPES OF EMPLOYMENT UNDER THE JURISDICTION OF AGMA

Agreement made this ____11th____ day of ____JUNE____, 19..40..

by and between the undersigned ARTIST, a member in good standing of the AMERICAN GUILD OF MUSICAL ARTISTS, INC. (hereinafter referred to as "AGMA"), and the undersigned Employer or Employers:

1. AGREEMENT OF EMPLOYMENT AND COMPENSATION. The EMPLOYER hereby engages the ARTIST to render services as ____BALLET DANCER____

(Singer, dancer, chorister, stage director, or in other capacity under the jurisdiction of AGMA)

in the company or production known as ____THE BALLET THEATRE____

(Name of Opera Company, Ballet Company, Concert Attraction, etc.)

for a period of ____ONE____ week(s), beginning on the ____27th____ day of ____JULY____, 19..40.., and ending upon one week's written notice of termination by either party to the other, but in no case shall this contract or the employment of the ARTIST hereunder be terminated earlier than the ____2nd____ day of ____AUGUST____, 19..40..

The EMPLOYER agrees to pay the ARTIST the sum of $..32.50.. per week during the above stated period for rendering the service stated above. The ARTIST hereby agrees to accept this employment upon the terms stated herein. The employment of the ARTIST hereunder shall be non-cancellable and continuous without lay-off or interruption. Compensation shall be paid in United States currency before 6 p.m. on the last day of each week.

2. DEDUCTIONS. The actual net compensation of the ARTIST shall be set forth herein and there shall be no remissions, rebate, discount, booking fee, commission or other payment or deduction whatsoever from the ARTIST's compensation except such taxes or withholdings as are required by statute, and except further that dues and initiation fees payable to AGMA shall be deducted from the compensation of the ARTIST and paid by the EMPLOYER to AGMA, and the ARTIST hereby authorizes the EMPLOYER to make such deduction and payment as AGMA directs. The EMPLOYER warrants that this clause will be fully and faithfully observed by himself and by any and all of his agents, representatives and employees.

they may hereafter be lawfully amended.

In the event that any collective bargaining agreement (BASIC AGREEMENT) exists between AGMA and the EMPLOYER containing provisions not included in AGMA RULES, or which modify any part or provision of AGMA RULES with respect to the employment of the ARTIST hereunder and specifically with respect to minimum rates of compensation and the proper manner and time of payment thereof, transportation of the ARTIST to and from the place or places of employment, etc., the provisions of such BASIC AGREEMENT shall, to the extent provided therein, be deemed part of this contract as though set forth in full.

The EMPLOYER further agrees (1) that he has notice that the ARTIST is a member of AGMA and must obey AGMA RULES, (2) that he will require the ARTIST to remain a member of AGMA in good standing throughout the duration of this contract, and (3) that he will not require the ARTIST to work in any company under his direction, management or control unless every ARTIST under the jurisdiction of AGMA employed in such company is a member of AGMA in good standing and remains so for the duration of his employment and only so long as the EMPLOYER has fully performed and is fully performing the covenants in each and every employment contract entered into, or hereafter during the term hereof entered into, with each and every AGMA member in each and every company operated and/or owned and/or controlled by him or with which he may be in any way connected.

4. NO WAIVERS OR CHANGES ALLOWED—"SCHEDULE A": The EMPLOYER and the ARTIST hereby mutually agree that no riders, changes or alterations of this printed form shall be made or agreed to by either the EMPLOYER or the ARTIST without the written consent of AGMA, and the EMPLOYER further agrees that no such rider, change or alteration shall be required of or deemed binding upon the ARTIST unless AGMA's consent has been certified by the duly authorized officer of AGMA upon the face of such rider, change or alteration.

Further provisions and agreements not set forth above in the printed portion of this contract, may be set forth under "Schedule A" below, and any terms so set forth are hereby made a part of this agreement. No such terms may be set forth which are less favorable to the ARTIST than (1) the printed provisions of this contract, (2) the provisions of AGMA RULES, and/or (3) the provisions of any BASIC AGREEMENT between the EMPLOYER and AGMA relating to this contract or the employment of the ARTIST hereunder.

The acceptance by the ARTIST of cash, checks or other forms of payment, or the deposit, or retaining of cash, checks or other forms of payment shall in no way affect the right of the ARTIST or of AGMA to insist upon full payment under this contract. The signing by the ARTIST of waivers or releases, or the deposit of checks or money orders under stipulations, letters, or other writings that such deposit is in full payment, or the like, shall be of no force or effect.

5. ARBITRATION. The EMPLOYER and the ARTIST hereby jointly and severally agree that any controversy or claim arising out of or relating to this contract or the breach thereof, shall be settled by Arbitration, in accordance with the Rules, then obtaining, of the American Arbitration Association (except as may otherwise be provided in AGMA Rules), and judgment upon the award rendered may be entered in the highest Court of the Forum, State or Federal, having jurisdiction.

6. LAWS GOVERNING. This agreement shall be subject to, be construed by, and the right of all parties thereto shall be determined by the Laws of the State of New York, except as may otherwise be provided.

7. LIABILITY. This contract shall be executed by the ARTIST and by the EMPLOYER. If the EMPLOYER or EMPLOYERS or any of them is a corporation, this agreement must be signed by the corporation and by an individual as an individual and not as a corporate officer, and in any event a person signing as an officer, agent or representative of a corporation agrees that his signature hereto binds him as an individual as well as such officer, agent or representative.

IN WITNESS WHEREOF we have executed this agreement as of the date first above set forth.

THE BALLET THEATRE

_____
EMPLOYER(s)

_____

Gala Performance, choreographed by Antony
Tudor for Ballet Theatre, 1941. Tudor is on
far left, next to him is Robbins. Ballerinas in
center are (from left) Nora Kaye, Miriam
Golden and Karen Conrad. To left of Nora
Kaye is Maria Karnilova, who later starred
in Robbins' *Fiddler on the Roof*.

Jerome Robbins and Rosella Hightower in the
Ballet Theatre production of *Helen of Troy*,
choreographed by David Lichine, 1942. Robbins
upstaged the ballerinas with the belly laughs
he got as Hermes munching an apple, one of
many comic bits he invented for himself.

"'One season, I was an idiot gypsy in everything, with boots and earrings and brown body makeup and nothing to do.' [I played] a sheaf of wheat, a dandelion, a Chinese coolie, and a drop of water."

left. Three-Cornered Hat, choreographed by Léonide Massine for Ballet Theatre, 1943. Robbins is performing the Miller, the role created by Massine.

above. Russian Soldier, choreographed by Mikhail Fokine for Ballet Theatre, 1942.

above. Ballet Theatre dancers taking an afternoon sun break during rehearsal period for performance at Lewisohn Stadium, New York City, summer of 1942. From left: Robbins, David Nillo, Donald Saddler, John Kriza.

above right. On tour with the Ballet Theatre company, summer of 1942. From left: Nicholas Orloff, Antony Tudor, Jerome Robbins, Maria Karnilova, Donald Saddler.

below right. Nora Kaye and Jerome Robbins cutting up with fellow dancers on tour with Ballet Theatre.

"We both liked each other's ideas and that was it. We were off and running.... [Lenny] was writing the music while I was touring ...and he would send me records...and then I'd either write or call him and say, 'Variation 3 is much too long,' or 'this is too fast,' or 'this is wonderful.' [The dancers were pals of mine and we rehearsed while on tour] in cellars, lobbies, gyms— any place I could find room. Someone later said, 'You never had your nose out of the score during the entire trip.'"

Story, plot and mood line of ballet. Time distance not exact. 1, entrance of sailors; 2, bar scene and drinking; 3, 1st girl's entrance; 4, 2nd girl's entrance; 5, reentrance of first group; 6, solo dances; 7, the fight; 8, discovery that girls are gone; 9, 3rd girl's entrance; 10, exit.

40

Graph for *Fancy Free*. In the early years of his career, Robbins created detailed scenarios for his ballets. With *Fancy Free* in particular, he needed to do so to interest a composer in collaborating on the project. He recounted later that the final ballet followed his graph and scenario remarkably closely.

"... I did [*Fancy Free*] during the war years, when the kinds of people I described in the ballet were all around us.... A sailor in New York had to be cocky. He wanted to appear not to be afraid of the city, especially if he came from out of town."

above. Advertisement for the Ballet Theatre production of *Fancy Free* at the old Metropolitan Opera House on Broadway between 39th and 40th Streets, New York City.

right. Jerome Robbins and Janet Reed in *Fancy Free*, 1944. Robbins based the personalities of the characters on himself and his fellow dancer pals in the Ballet Theatre company. Robbins did not fight in the war because his draft status was 4-F, due to asthma.

"It was a surprise to all of us. [While we were rehearsing *Fancy Free*] no one had paid much attention....we were rather left alone. And I think a [Sol] Hurok press agent came and watched it, and then went back to Hurok and said, 'I think you're in for something here.' But we didn't know that and the ballet opened and we did our best...then came this reaction which was about the wildest reaction I've ever had for any ballet that I've ever done.... We had about twenty-two curtain calls, which is really extraordinary....

"...the ballet was...not scheduled to be performed again for another ten days. By that time, all the reviews had come in, and all the attention had come in. And when we got on the stage the second time, we were so nervous we more or less fell down on the stage and did all the wrong things."

"...everything really changed when my first ballet, *Fancy Free,* opened. Me, my career, my parents. They even changed their name to Robbins."

Rex Cooper, Janet Reed and Jerome Robbins in *Fancy Free*, 1944.

3

EARLY BALLET
BREAKING THE MOLD
1944–1957

"Balanchine...made me see that the work was more important than the success...that work in progress was what mattered most.... He wanted to get me not to worry about making a masterpiece every time. 'Just keep making ballets,' he used to say, 'and every once in a while one will be a masterpiece.'"

George Balanchine and Lincoln Kirsten. Kirsten was Balanchine's primary supporter and instrumental in the creation of the New York City Ballet.

Following *Fancy Free,* Robbins found himself coping with the pressure of instant acclaim. His print interviews during this time often emphasize the baffling adjustment to his new status as dance "genius." One day he was just another dancer, the next day he was supposed to have expert opinions on all subjects. He received invitations to shows where before he "couldn't afford to buy a ticket." Scripts were "suddenly being thrown" at him. He was elated but also aware of the irony of his sudden change in status.

Robbins was surprised, too, by another side effect of his success. He discovered that having done a successful "jazz" ballet, he was instantly typecast as that "jazz choreographer." With a career marked by fluid movement between ballet and commercial theater, Robbins would fight this typecasting and resist categorization his whole life.

Fortunately, he was always brimming over with ambitious plans, and Robbins plunged ahead with new projects for Ballet Theatre. After *Fancy Free,* he choreographed and danced in the light and comic *Interplay* (1945) and then *Facsimile* (1946), which he described as his first venture into the "serious and the sad" and "a step forward for me whether it comes out successfully or not."

In 1948, at the age of thirty, he wrote a fan letter to George Balanchine. He had just seen Balanchine's *Symphony in C* featuring ballerinas Maria Tallchief and Tanaquil Le Clercq, "and I absolutely fell in love with it…and thought, 'Oh boy, I want to work with that company.'" He offered to perform, choreograph, whatever was needed—to which Balanchine said, "Come."

In his early years at New York City Ballet, Robbins was often a featured dancer, quite amazing considering everything else he was doing both in ballet and theater. He performed in Balanchine's *Bourrée Fantasque* (1949) with Tanaquil Le Clercq. In 1950, Balanchine revived *Prodigal Son* with Robbins in the title role and in 1951 created *Tyl Ulenspiegel* especially for Robbins. While he enjoyed dancing *Prodigal Son,* Robbins found *Tyl*…very hard. It was a short ballet, with many prop and costume changes and little actual dancing, and the dancers

"...within a year [Balanchine] made me associate artistic director, and I felt his blessing on my work, his interest, his help—I always showed my work to him and listened carefully to his responses. Just to watch his work is enough of an example for any choreographer to learn."

New York City Ballet rehearsal of *Prodigal Son,* 1950, choreographed by Balanchine, who is standing by the piano. Robbins is supporting Maria Tallchief.

Jerome Robbins (center) in *Tyl Ulenspiegel*, 1951, choreographed by Balanchine, music by Richard Strauss. The spectacular set was designed by Estaban Francés and was irreparably destroyed in a fire.

Age of Anxiety, based on a W.H. Auden poem, with a score by Leonard Bernstein, 1950. From left: Todd Bolender, Tanaquil Le Clercq, Jerome Robbins and Roy Tobias.

Age of Anxiety, 1950.

"The problem of the artist is—how can this be interpreted anew and artistically, with fresh and additional insight? What is my contribution in handling this material? How can these particular characters express themselves so that people will believe what they are saying?"

Jerome Robbins taking a bow at City Center
with the cast of *The Guests,* his first ballet
choreographed for New York City Ballet,
1949. Front from left: Nicholas Magallanes,
Maria Tallchief, Jerome Robbins and Marc
Blitzstein (composer).

"...my first ballet for the company...was *The Guests,* which George [Balanchine] called 'The Cluded.' And I asked him, 'Why do you call it that?' He said, 'Oh, it's about the included and the excluded.' And he was right."

"George started his rehearsal [for *Jones Beach*] in one studio, and I was working on something else in another. After he had created I don't know how many bars he took a break, came to me and said, 'Come and take a look.'

"They ran through what he had done, and then he said, 'Now go on.' 'What do you mean?' I asked. 'Just go on from there,' he said. It was like being in a duel, having a rapier thrown for you to catch and having to defend yourself."

below. Maria Tallchief and Jerome Robbins posing downstage in *Jones Beach,* 1950, co-choreographed by George Balanchine and Robbins for New York City Ballet. Joint choreographies are rare, but Robbins and Balanchine worked well together. The bathing suits for the ballet were supplied by Jantzen.

left. The Mosquito ballet shown here is a section Robbins choreographed.

The New York City Ballet production of
Robbins' fascinating and disturbing *The Cage*,
1951, choreographed to Igor Stravinsky's
String Concerto in D.

"I had the score [for *The Cage*]
for about a year and a half, two
years.... I kept playing it, and I
thought, '...I know there's a
dramatic line in it somewhere or
other.' And then I read a story
about the Amazons, and I thought,
'Why don't I do it about the
Amazons?'

So I started it. And I got about
halfway through the first movement and...I thought, 'This is
terrible.... I've got to do better
than that.' So I kept reading
and then I stumbled on material
about insects and their prey. And
I thought, 'Now that I think I can
handle. There's a little twist. It's
a little offbeat.' So I started that
way, and bang, it just went like
a dream."

Tanaquil Le Clercq and Francisco Moncion in *Afternoon of a Faun*, City Center, May 14, 1953. After Robbins showed set designer Jean Rosenthal a drawing by Paul Cadmus of dancers in a studio, Rosenthal designed this spectacular set.

"*The Concert* goes back to my childhood when a musical piece was briefly explained to me [as] 'Butterflies,' 'Raindrops' and so on…. I allowed myself to introduce into [the piece] my own personal touch of madness, but it conceals a deeper meaning which I only discovered when I had finished composing it: in the short anecdotes…there are no victors. Through the music, all the characters abandon their every-day selves. Whether they move up or down, they all try to do something extraordinary but they are all defeated by circumstances which inevitably bring them back to earth."

The deliciously comic *The Concert (Or the Perils of Everybody)*, 1956, was a particular favorite of Robbins' and always popular in the New York City Ballet repertoire.

"The fascination of choreography is...when you start a ballet, it's in an empty studio...and the first dancer begins—it's rather an awesome moment because it's like putting the first mark of ink on a piece of blank paper.... Because from then on, your whole pattern is going to be connected to that. Your whole structure. I always feel choreography is a little like building a bridge, which is that you start on one side, and you build a step, and then you build another step, and another step, and the bridge is sort of arced out over nothing, and the structure of it has to contain itself so that it meets at the end of the ballet and makes an architectural structure which is satisfying."

Jerome Robbins rehearsing with dancer
Wilma Curley.

4

MASTERING THE CRAFT

1944–1957

"Oh, here we go again. People always insist on it being one way or the other. When I was on Broadway, I was 'that ballet man.' In ballet, I was 'that Broadway man.' It's not [a matter of] pitting one against the other. Each world fertilized the other. The work I did on *King and I* spilled over into my ballet, *The Cage*. Work on *Look, Ma, I'm Dancin'!* helped me make *The Concert*."

Jerome Robbins working with a ballet score in his apartment at 154 East 74th Street, New York City.

"I didn't realize how deep the water was going to be [in transposing *Fancy Free* into another medium], and I waded right in, arms flailing. All that went on was cut and re-do, cut and re-do. It was lacerating."

It seemed a natural idea to turn the wildly successful *Fancy Free* into a Broadway show, and set designer Oliver Smith persuaded Robbins and Leonard Bernstein to expand the ballet into a musical. Bernstein brought in his friends Betty Comden and Adolph Green to write the book and lyrics, and not long after the opening of the ballet, Robbins found himself choreographing his first show for Broadway, *On The Town.* It would prove to be an intense learning experience for all involved. Robbins had only danced in the chorus of a few Broadway musicals, and the rest of the participants had no real experience on Broadway before then. Robbins said that he literally learned on his feet.

It was on this show that Robbins met George Abbott, who directed. Abbott loved dance of any kind and loved to dance himself, particularly ballroom dancing, which he did frequently right up to his last years past the age of 100. He was a willing mentor to Robbins and greatly respected the choreographer's special talent. All in all, Abbott and Robbins did six shows together: *On The Town, Billion Dollar Baby, High Button Shoes* and *Call Me Madam,* for which Abbott directed and Robbins choreographed, and *Look, Ma, I'm Dancin'!* and *The Pajama Game,* which they co-directed. Robbins spoke to me of Abbott with great affection, describing a giant, fatherly figure who was cool, decisive and supremely self-confident—all traits that Robbins sometimes wished for himself.

Even in so-called "light-hearted" works, Robbins took his craft seriously. His underlying purpose was always serious. As early as 1948, he was considering the possibility of combining

Leonard Bernstein and Jerome Robbins
during a rehearsal for *On The Town*, 1944. The
"boy wonders" are both 26 in this photograph.

the entertainment value and wide audience appeal of the musical format with a deeper, more personal subject matter. It was both a gift and a curse for Robbins that he never liked to repeat himself. In addition to moving back and forth between ballet and Broadway, he was always looking to extend the boundaries and possibilities within these existing venues. In 1949, he had an idea for just such a show—but it would take eight years for it to arrive on Broadway as *West Side Story.*

Despite the prominence of Robbins, Leonard Bernstein and Arthur Laurents (Stephen Sondheim was then an unknown), it was difficult to find a producer for the project. Robbins was remarkable sanguine about the early rejections. "Every time the script came back to us," he said, "we would look it over to see how we could improve it. Perhaps that's why it turned out as well as it did." The project nearly sank altogether when one of the producers pulled out at the last minute, having decided that the show was too depressing and certain to fail. *West Side Story* finally premiered at the Winter Garden Theatre in New York City on September 26, 1957.

Given that it has become one of the most admired and acclaimed musicals of the twentieth century, it is surprising to discover that the reviews the following day were hardly raves. In fact, though most reviewers admired the choreography in particular, they seemed unable to come to terms with how different this show was from musicals they had seen before and with the fact that its ending was so tragic. It is even more surprising to discover that most of these critics did not consider the songs either memorable or hummable. It was only four years later, when the film version was released, that *West Side Story* began to take its powerful place in the popular imagination.

With its inter-ethnic tensions, its intra-cultural struggles to hold on to Old World values and its tragic love affair, *West Side Story* mined Robbins' deepest creative themes. These themes also struck a deep and resonating chord in people all over the world, and this timeless show continues to build new audiences every year.

Sono Osato and Jerome Robbins rehearsing
On The Town, 1944. Osato played the role of
Miss Subways.

above. On the Town, 1945

left. From left: Leonard Bernstein
(composer), Adolph Green and Betty Comden
(book/lyric writers) and Jerome Robbins
(choreographer) working in *On The Town,* 1944.

Look, ma, I'm an autobiography!

Jerome Robbins, a Broadway wonder, has dreamed up a dansical comedy based on his life

By Selma Robinson

m6   Jerome Robbins danced the role of The Boy in his newest ballet, *Summer Day*, at its City Center debut recently.

WHEN *Look, Ma, I'm Dancing*, a new musical, is presented here next month by George Abbott, its program will read something like this: "Conceived by Jerome Robbins. Dances and choreography by Mr. Robbins. Staged by Mr. Abbott and Mr. Robbins."

This Jerome Robbins, a thin, dark, intense young man, just turned 29, is the same fellow who created the show-stopping Mack Sennett ballet in *High Button Shoes;* the same who kidded the Charleston and the old-time movie heroes in *Billion Dollar Baby;* who did the dances for *On the Town*, a smash hit of a few seasons ago; who choreographed and danced in *Fancy Free*, one of the most successful ballets in recent years.

The new show, *Look, Ma, I'm Dancing*, is best described as a dansical. It's about a young choreographer who crashes into ballet by way of the borscht circuit, kicks the traditional ballet in the teeth and establishes himself as an overnight success, just as he expected.

It was inevitable

Jerry Robbins, too, played the borscht, staging ballets for adult camps; some of his ballets kid such classics as *Scheherazade* and *Sylphides*, and he, too, has always counted on success. But *Look, Ma* is only quasi-autobiographical. Unlike his brassy, ruthless hero, Jerry is shy and self-effacing, confident but very sensitive for his success, crammed into space of three and a half year[s] inevitable," says ballerina [...] of his oldest friends, and [...] right on being successful [...] full of talent."

Early dancing lessons in the [...] family went to Sonya, Jerry's older [...] and she gave him a few pointers in [...] home in Weehawken, N. J. Jerry showed a decided talent for the piano, his mother remembers. His real life's work, however, was to be chemistry, and he enrolled at NYU.

Jerry left NYU at the age of 16 to study dancing with Ella Dagonova. He paid for his three lessons a week by washing her windows and doing small bits in the Yiddish theater.

Long before he tried his hand at choreography he danced in all the standard ballets: he was a eunuch in *Scheherazade*, a gypsy in *Aleko*, a sheaf of wheat, a snowflake, a peasant, and a French courtier. After these ignominious classic roles, it is not surprising that in his most recent ballet, *Summer Day*, he gently satirizes the classic Russian Ballet by presenting it from a child's point of view.

Nice, even gallop

Robbins was graduated into leading roles by the Ballet Theatre, which cast him in modern ballets like those of Agnes de Mille as well as the traditional pieces.

His own tastes run to stuff as contemporaneous as radio and swing. *Fancy Free*, which had its debut in the war year of 1944, was about three young sailors on the make, lonesome, exuberant, inoffensively vulgar. He counted on its being a hit. "It couldn't fail because too many people could understand and appreciate it," he explained.

At about that time, the ballet manager's representative, a little apprehensive about the proportions of Jerry's ambitions, told me privately: "Jerry's giddy with his success. He'll settle down to a nice even gait when this all dies down."

Robbins *has* settled down—to a nice, even gallop that includes three ballets and four major Broadway musicals. He drives around in a cream-colored Dodge convertible, two-thirds of it a gift from the grateful producers of *High Button Shoes*, and he has moved from his Village flat to a five-room apartment on Park Avenue.

"As you see, it's a walk-up," Jerry consoled me as I reached his door on the to[p] floor to interview him recently.

This article on *Look, Ma, I'm Dancin'!* is from the newspaper *PM*, December 21, 1947. The photograph is of Robbins dancing in *Summer Day*, choreographed for Ballet Theatre in 1947.

"[*Look Ma, I'm Dancin'!*] is a ballet about the yearnings and hopes and dreams of teen-age kids, about all the things that combine to make a boy like Eddie obsessed with a desire for success ... it's a commentary on the Sad Generation. It's the feeling, the music, the tempo of the kids who grew up in the Twenties and Thirties, and are becoming men and women in the Forties."

Look, Ma, I'm Dancin'!, 1948. From left: Katharine Sergava, Nancy Walker, Harold Lang (as Eddie Winkler), Janet Reed, Alice Pearce, Conductor (unidentified). In addition to doing the choreography, Robbins co-directed with George Abbott and received credit for conceiving the show. Robbins used his experiences at Ballet Theatre as background for the story.

The Sleepwalkers ballet, from *Look, Ma, I'm Dancin'!*, 1948.

"I did a Sleepwalkers ballet, which took place on a train at night in which everyone was having a letch with someone else.... Rather than being caught, they were pretending they were sleepwalking. It started very rashly and built up to people high on each other's shoulders, still sleep-walking. It was not a long [ballet], but it was a good one."

"A producer says, 'We want you but we don't want any ballet. We want a number like the Charleston in *Billion Dollar Baby*.' 'But, that's ballet,' I tell him. 'Yes,' he says, 'but we don't want any ballet.' ...I've tried to break down the iron-clad traditional forms of both musical comedy and ballet. I think *Fancy Free* moved ballet toward the theater and that *Billion Dollar Baby* moved theater toward ballet— or maybe you'd better call it dance movement."

The Charleston ballet from *Billion Dollar Baby*, 1945. Book and lyrics by Adolph Green and Betty Comden; music by Morton Gould; directed by George Abbott.

ALONG BROADWAY · High spot of the show is the Mack Sennett ballet, a hilarious mixture of up-to-date choreography, Keystone cops, robbers, bathing beauties a la 1914 and an ape. HIGH BUTTON SHOES
(NEWS foto by _____ and _____)

"[When I read the script for *High Button Shoes*], I said, 'Here's a chance to do a Mack Sennett ballet.' It just jumped to my mind. It had to be manipulated into the plot so that [the characters] Floy and Mamo could be arrested. For my research I went to the Museum of Modern Art, saw a lot of old movies of Chester Conklin and Mack Swain and consulted a lot of old dancers.

"First I had to get the style and then I had to distort it. If I had done it exactly as it had been done then it might look tame, might even be boring. It's like furniture. You don't furnish your home exactly as the Victorians did, for instance. You combine it with modern stuff to spike it up or to give it emphasis."

above. The Mack Sennett ballet in *High Button Shoes,* 1947, featuring bathing beauties and Keystone cops and robbers. This ballet was a smash hit at the time, cementing Robbins' reputation as a dance genius

left. Jerome Robbins on the set of *High Button Shoes,* 1947, for which he did the choreography. Music by Jule Styne; lyrics by Sammy Cahn; directed by George Abbott.

"If certain people had been told...that my Atlantic City Bath House number and the other dances in that show were ballets, they'd have been scared to come to the theater. And if they had enjoyed a number and later had been told it was a ballet, they wouldn't have admitted that they liked it."

"Everyone else concerned with creating a show can do so in privacy, but when it comes to my part of the business, I can only assimilate the musical idea and the setting and then wait till I am on stage with my dancers before I get going. Every show brings its own problems and solutions. All one carries from one job to the next is an increasing amount of craft, patience, flexibility and the knowledge that whether one was successful or not in the last show has no bearing on the way the current job is going to turn out."

Jerome Robbins rehearsing Allyn McLerie and Tommy Rall in *Miss Liberty,* 1949. Music and lyrics by Irving Berlin; book by Robert E. Sherwood; directed by Moss Hart.

The Caboose ballet from *Miss Liberty*, 1949.

"...In Philadelphia while *Miss Liberty* was trying out...one night I went to a nightclub with Irving Berlin, Moss Hart, Robert Sherwood and a few others from the show. The club owner heard we were there and he announced each of us to the audience. Everybody, of course, knew Berlin. They applauded him wildly. Then Sherwood and Hart were introduced. And the audience cheered them. But when my name was mentioned all I heard around me was 'What the devil is a choreographer?'"

Jerome Robbins with *Call Me Madam* producer Leland Hayward and composer Irving Berlin, 1950. Robbins was a close friend of Hayward and his then wife, Nancy "Slim" Hayward.

right. Jerome Robbins and George Abbott (director) in rehearsal for *Call Me Madam*, 1950. Music and lyrics by Irving Berlin; book by Howard Lindsay and Russel Crouse.

"I first worked with Mr. Abbott on *On the Town.* We were out of town for ten whole days, it was my first show, I was totally a novice doing a Broadway show. I liked the work I had done in rehearsal very much, but found it didn't work in the context of the show. This threw me. Mr. Abbott was clear and helpful in editing and suggesting cuts, in clipping a ballet in half and putting it in two places in the show. He was very skillful and very helpful, and decisive."

The stage version of *The King and I*, 1951.
Music by Richard Rodgers; book and lyrics
by Oscar Hammerstein II; directed by John
Van Druten. The Small House of Uncle
Thomas ballet that Robbins created for the
show tackled the serious subject of slavery
and remains an enduring jewel.

right. Two's Company, 1952, a revue starring
Bette Davis and dancer Nora Kaye. Robbins
later told me that there were many good
things in the show—including, intermittently,
Bette Davis' performance—but she was not
comfortable on stage and the show closed
shortly after opening.

above. A dance with ribbons Jerome Robbins
created for *Two's Company*, 1952.

Walter Winchell Says.

TIMES
Jan 4/53

"**BETTE DAVIS**
DELIGHTFUL IN
TWO'S COMPANY
BEST OF THE BEST!

SEE Bette Davis shake the shimmy and wiggle her wiggle section.

SEE Bette Davis the Hollywood star, steal the top scenes again.

SEE Bette Davis and her delightful cast at the Alvin.

THE BREEZIEST REVUE IN TOWN!"

THE NEW MUSICAL HIT!

with HIRAM
SHERMAN • DAVID
BURNS • NORA
KAYE

Choreography by **JEROME ROBBINS**

MAIL ORDERS GIVEN PROMPT ATTENTION

Evgs. Orch. $7.20; Mezz. $6.00; Balc. $4.80, 4.20, 3.60, 3.00, 2.40.
Mats. Wednesday & Saturday: Orch. $4.20; Mezz. $3.60; Balc. $3.00,
2.40, 1.80. Tax Included. Please enclose stamped, self-addressed
envelope. Kindly specify several alternate dates.

ALVIN THEATRE, 250 W. 52nd St., N. Y. 19

The following performances are completely sold out: Evgs., Jan. 6, 7,
8, 12, 13, 14, 15, 20, 21, 26, 28, 29. Feb. 3, 4, 11, 25. March 4, 21.

139

above. May 5, 1953. Jerome Robbins appears
before the Committee on Un-American
Activities of the House of Representatives at
the Federal Courthouse in New York City.
He testifies that he joined the Communist
party's Theatrical Transient Group on
Christmas in 1943, because he thought the
party was fighting racism, fascism and
anti-Semitism, and that he became disillu-
sioned and quit in 1947.

right. A page in Robbins' journal, 1976. In
this collage, Robbins blanked out his face
in a photograph, a painful indication of his
struggle with his identity.

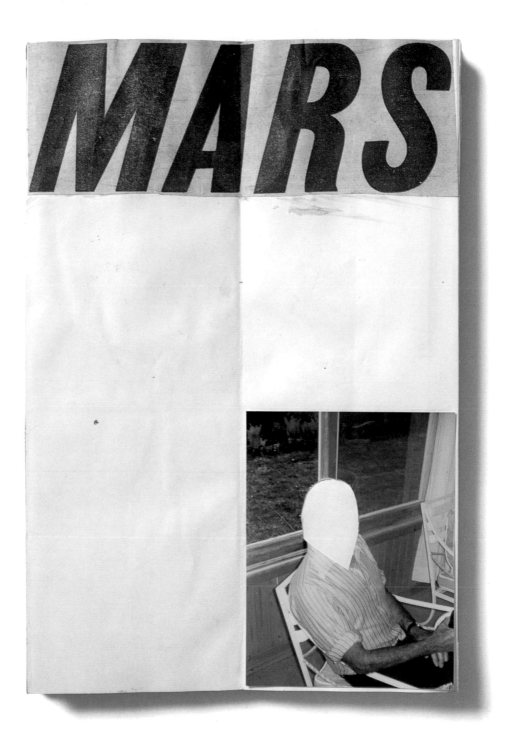

The curtain call for *The Pajama Game,* which
premiered in 1954. Co-directed with George
Abbott, it was the last of the six shows they
worked on together. Robbins hired Bob Fosse
to do the choreography, giving Fosse his
first major break in the theater.

143

"I'm in love...with the live stage. It's my first and only love. Movies? I'm fascinated by the medium but not by Hollywood."

Jerome Robbins directing Mary Martin
in *Peter Pan,* 1954.

Robbins and Mary Martin "flying" on the set of the television version of *Peter Pan*, 1955.

A rehearsal meeting of the creative team and chorus girls for *Bells Are Ringing,* as appeared in the *New York Times,* September 16, 1956. Robbins (director, in back with pencil) and, seated from left, Bob Fosse (choreographer), Adolph Green (book and lyrics), Judy Holliday (star), Betty Comden (book and lyrics) and Jule Styne (music).

"BELLS ARE RINGING"——Chorus girls for the new Judy Holliday musical line up for instruction. They face, left to right, choreographer Bob Fosse, co-author Adolph

Times Sept 16/56

director Jerome Robbins, Miss Holliday, co-author Betty Comden and composer Jule Styne. Miss
y will portray an operator for a telephone answering service. A Nov. 29 prospect at the Shubert.

Stephen Sondheim, Leonard Bernstein and
Jerome Robbins meeting about *West Side
Story*, December 1956.

"I don't like to theorize about how or if the show changed future musicals. For me what was important about *West Side Story* was our *aspiration.* I wanted to find out at that time how far we, as 'long-haired artists,' could go in bringing our crafts and talents to a musical. Why did we have to do it separately and elsewhere? Why did Lenny have to write an opera, Arthur a play, me a ballet? Why couldn't we, in aspiration, try to bring our deepest talents together to the commercial theater in this work? That was the true *gesture* of the show."

"There was this wonderful mutual exchange going on.... we gave to each other, took from each other, yielded to each other, surrendered, reworked, put back together again.... It was a very important and extraordinary time."

"…somewhere around 1949…this friend of mine [Montgomery Clift] was offered the role of Romeo. He said to me, 'This part seems very passive, would you tell me what you think I should do with it?' So I asked myself, 'If I were to play this, how would I make it come to life?' I tried to imagine it in terms of today. That clicked in, and I said to myself, 'There's a wonderful idea here.'"

"…the idea came to me of a *Romeo and Juliet* among the gangs of New York. Originally, it was to be set on the lower East Side, among the Italians and Irish, but while we were working on it suddenly things blew up in the city, and my collaborators Arthur Laurents and Leonard Bernstein had the idea to change it to the Puerto Ricans on the West Side."

above right. Creative team for *West Side Story,* 1957. From left: Stephen Sondheim (lyrics), Arthur Laurents (book), Harold Prince (co-producer), Robert E. Griffith (co-producer), Leonard Bernstein (music), Jerome Robbins (choreographer and director).

right. Rehearsal for *West Side Story,* 1957. From left: Leonard Bernstein, Arthur Laurents, Jerome Robbins, Irene Sharaff (costume designer), Stephen Sondheim, Robert E. Griffith and Ruth Mitchell (stage manager).

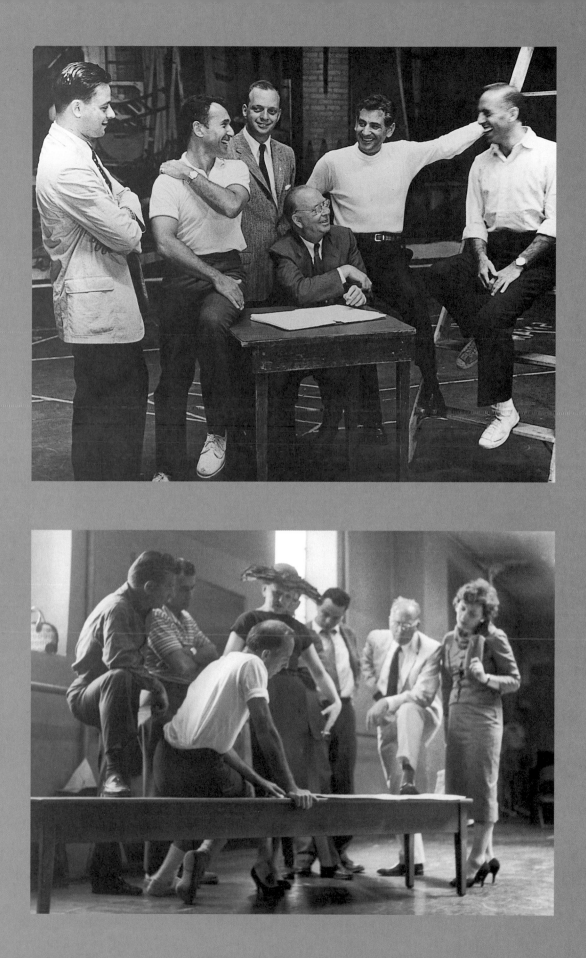

"I am a perfectionist.... I wear that badge proudly. I think that's what art is about—trying to make it as good as you possibly can.... People gripe. They gripe. I can't help what they say.... My idea is to do a show and put it in front of the people and make it as good as I can and as good as I think it should be."

Jerome Robbins with Tom Abbott at a
rehearsal for *West Side Story*, 1957. Abbott
worked with Robbins for many years after
as an assistant, frequently staging the dances
of *West Side Story* road companies.

155

A rehearsal for *West Side Story* in the Chester Hale Studio above a garage on West 56th Street near Carnegie Hall . From left: Robert E. Griffith, Harold Prince, Jerome Robbins, Stephen Sondheim, Leonard Bernstein, Arthur Laurents, Gerald Freedman, Ruth Mitchell, Larry Kert.

"...we could not get anyone to produce [*West Side Story*]. It took us about three years of peddling it around.... No one would even touch it. They didn't like the score, they didn't like the idea, they didn't like what it was about. They didn't like anything about it."

"...we kept going back to the...play, saying, 'That didn't work, I wonder why not, what didn't they like, let's take a look at it again.' ...I'm glad we didn't get *West Side Story* on right away. Between the time we thought of it and finally did it, we did an immense amount of work on it."

Rehearsal of *West Side Story* gang members, 1957. Robbins employed what some saw as a Method-acting approach when rehearsing the dancers by encouraging them to paper the walls of the rehearsal room with images of New York gang life and discouraging the Sharks and Jets from intermingling at rehearsals and on their own time, in or out of the theater. From left: Jay Norman, Ronald Lee, Tom Abbott, Howard Jeffrey, Jerome Robbins, Grover Dale.

Jerome Robbins directing Wilma Curley,
Mickey Calin and other chorus members in a
rehearsal of *West Side Story*, 1957.

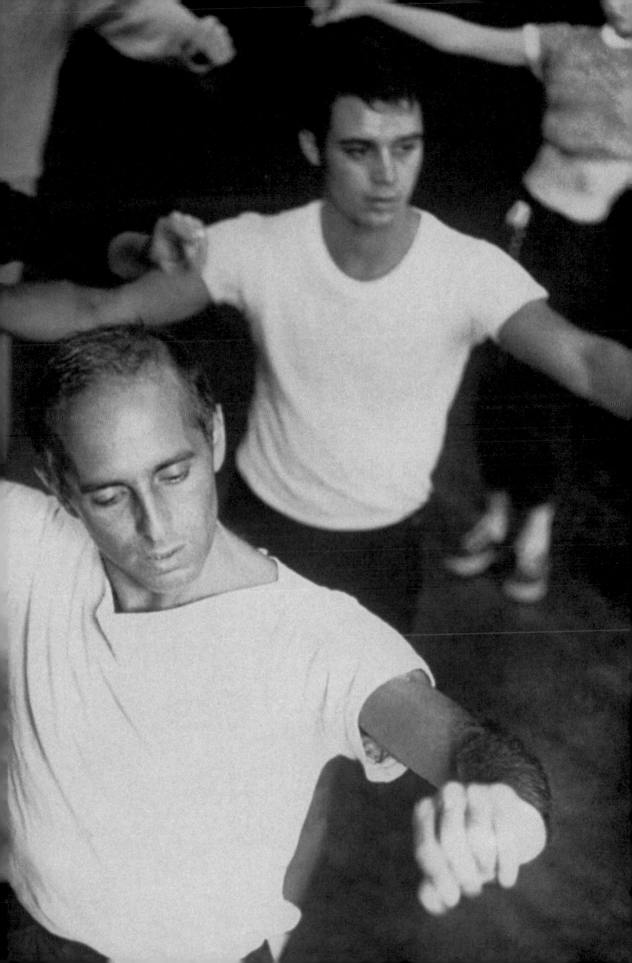

"We all thought *West Side Story* was just a temporary title we'd discard once someone came up with a better one. Yet no one ever did."

West Side Story.

From left: Carmen Guiterrez, Lynn Ross, Chita Rivera, Elizabeth Taylor in *West Side Story*, 1957.

A touring company of *West Side Story*.

Jerome Robbins posing with trunks to pro-
mote tour of his ballet company, Ballets
U.S.A. Created originally for the 1958 Festival
of Two Worlds in Spoleto, Italy, the company
received such an enthusiastic critical and
audience response that it toured Europe and
played a season in New York.

5

CULMINATION
THE MERGING OF DANCE AND STORY
1957–1965

"Everything has a chance of failure. The riskiest thing, the most treacherous thing, is to do something you don't want to do."

Big money and star power are great temptations, but when the elements don't mesh, what at first looks like an absolute sure thing can turn into an instant flop. The good and bad news about success is that it breeds many choices. After *West Side Story,* Robbins was one of the most highly sought-after artists in musical theater. Through earlier experiences, he'd learned that even when a show looked good on paper and featured a star (as with Bette Davis in *Two's Company*) or a creative team (as

with Moss Hart, Robert Sherwood and Irving Berlin in *Miss
Liberty*) that he particularly respected, it did not guarantee a hit.
Although he admired Bette Davis "extravagantly," *Two's
Company* had been a disappointment. By the late 1950s, Robbins
was clearer about the need to choose material that resonated
with his deeper instincts.

As it was his nature to continuously challenge himself
artistically, his work began to take on more variety. In 1958, he
formed his own company, Ballets U.S.A., to perform his ballets
at the Festival of Two Worlds in Spoleto, Italy. The company was
received so well, it went on to tour Europe and then danced on
Broadway for a season.

Robbins also found himself in great demand as a "play
doctor." He liked to solve problems and was good at it, becoming
intrigued by the many troubles that can besiege a production.
A Funny Thing Happened On the Way to the Forum (1962) was
floundering before Robbins came in and restaged—uncredited
—some of the numbers, putting in the opening number, "Comedy
Tonight," which successfully turned around a show that had
been billed as a comedy but was not getting laughs.

As time went on, though, Robbins was less and less seduced
by a producer's cries for help. He had already gotten his feet wet
in film—choreographing with his usual technical perfectionism
the Small House of Uncle Thomas ballet for the movie version of
The King and I. The ballet has lost none of its impact today and
remains a glistening jewel.

But Robbins' notorious perfectionism became an issue on
the film version of *West Side Story.* As Co-Director in 1960,
he enjoyed the actual work and the results are electrifying in the
finished movie, but he was let go from the production before
completion. Robbins later felt that he had been made the fall guy
for budget problems by people who didn't understand what was
involved in filming a musical, and his mixed feelings were never
fully appeased by the Oscars he received for his work.

"I believe very strongly that ballet dancing in America, originally an imported product…, has been completely influenced and drastically changed by the culture in which it has grown up. We in America dress, eat, think, talk and walk differently from any other people. We also dance differently…. Ballets U.S.A. was planned to show Europeans the variety of techniques, styles and theatrical approaches that are America's particular development in dance."

Ballets U.S.A. rehearsals, 1958–1959.

Robbins began looking for new challenges in the theater, outside the world of musical comedy. He took on an ambitious production of Bertolt Brecht's *Mother Courage and Her Children* (1963), but his work fell short of his expectations. He had greater success with an off-Broadway play written by Arthur Kopit, *Oh Dad, Poor Dad, Mama's Hung You in the Closet and I'm Feelin' So Sad* (1962).

More often than not, Robbins' greatest achievements came from ideas he generated himself, as with *Fancy Free* and *West Side Story*. One day, however, composer Sheldon Harnick and lyric writer Jerry Bock brought Robbins a project based on the stories of Sholem Aleichem, which would become *Fiddler on the Roof* (1964). It was a story of a small Jewish community in a town in Russia at the turn of the century. Robbins was deeply moved by the score, and the idea had powerful resonance

Rehearsing dancer Erin Martin in *Moves,* 1959.

"As I go along, I seem to start to get a sense of what [a piece] is about. Sometimes I'm very surprised by where I begin and end up. That's why I can't understand how people can say, 'Oh, I do the ending first.' I can't do that. I have to get to it by the logic of what the choreography leads to."

Jerome Robbins was an accomplished photographer and had his own darkroom. He
often photographed his own ballets. *Moves*,
danced by Ballets U.S.A., appeared in *Dance
Magazine*, June 1961.

DANC

The fourth movement, which consists of several sets of pas de deux, above, leads to a group finale.

END

Opposite and above: "Pas de Deux," a sequence from "Moves." Performed here by Michael Maule and Erin Martin, it will be seen this year with Scott Douglas and Miss Martin.

"I had commissioned a score from Aaron Copland for Ballets U.S.A. He was late writing it while I was already in rehearsal, so I'd go to Aaron and he'd play me a piece that he'd composed and I'd leave the rehearsal with some of the tunes and certainly the rhythm in my head. So I started to choreograph it even though there was no real score...and suddenly I looked at it and I thought, 'This is very interesting without any music.' And so I went ahead and choreographed the whole ballet in silence...called *Moves*."

for him. Here was a chance to create a work for the stage that would mine the rich vein of his own Jewish heritage, for which he had so many conflicting emotions.

In his usual fashion, Robbins prepared strenuously, immersing himself in Jewish lore and going into the Hasidic community in New York to research his dances. Not only did he want the dances to be authentic, he wanted them to appear as if they were simply extensions of normal human behavior and not separate "dance numbers."

Fiddler on the Roof was a huge success. In its time, it was the longest running play on Broadway, and Robbins received two Tonys, one for choreography and one for direction. With *Fiddler...* he had reached the pinnacle of his desire to blur the boundaries between dance and story. But reaching a pinnacle always contains within itself an ending, even if not completely acknowledged at the time.

New York Export: Opus Jazz, choreographed for Ballets U.S.A., 1958. Robbins always hoped to revive this ballet with another company, but never achieved this goal.

The Umbrella ballet in the Ballets U.S.A.
production of *The Concert*, 1958.

Rehearsing the Umbrella ballet, 1958.

"...I like accidents and I like to use them. My eyes are always alert to the breaking of a rule. This can be exciting. It is rather like a large piece of crystal in which you look for a crack. Perfection itself is dull....

"I want my intentions performed, but these include the use of accidents. It is not perfection to repeat something correctly and automatically. Perfection is to be found in recreating, renewing, refreshing."

Drop by Saul Steinberg designed for the
Ballets U.S.A. version of *The Concert*, 1958.

Jerome Robbins and his Ballets U.S.A. company. Photographer Phillippe Halsman was well-known for taking photographs of his subjects jumping.

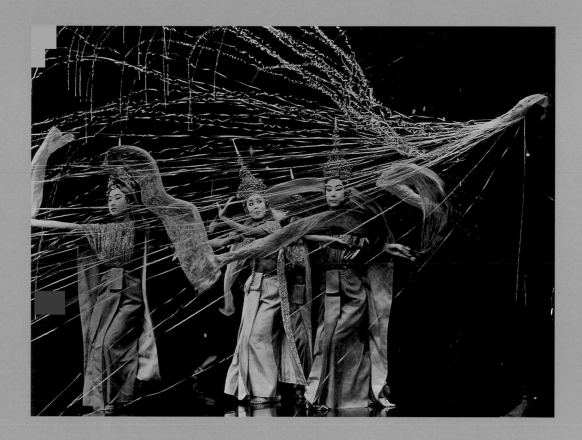

left. The King and I, film version, 1956.

above. Rain ballet, *The King and I,* 1956.

The King and I, 1956.

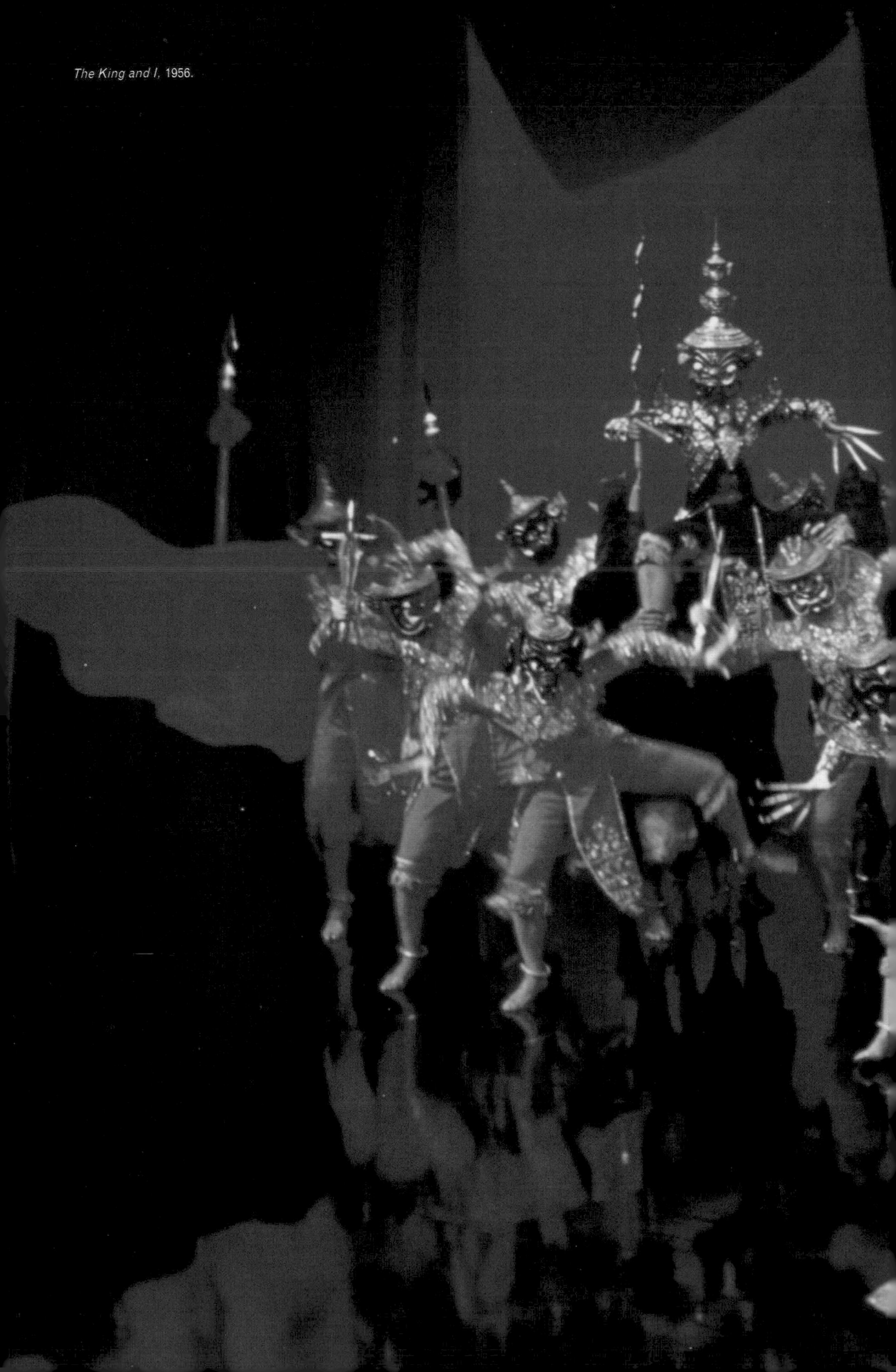

"My father was always asking me, 'When are you going to Hollywood?' He'd ask me that no matter what success I had elsewhere. Finally I did *The King and I*. I got him tickets to the fancy opening night premiere and told him to watch for my name on the screen. The next day, I asked him how he liked the movie, especially my dances. All he said was: 'When are you going to do another one?'"

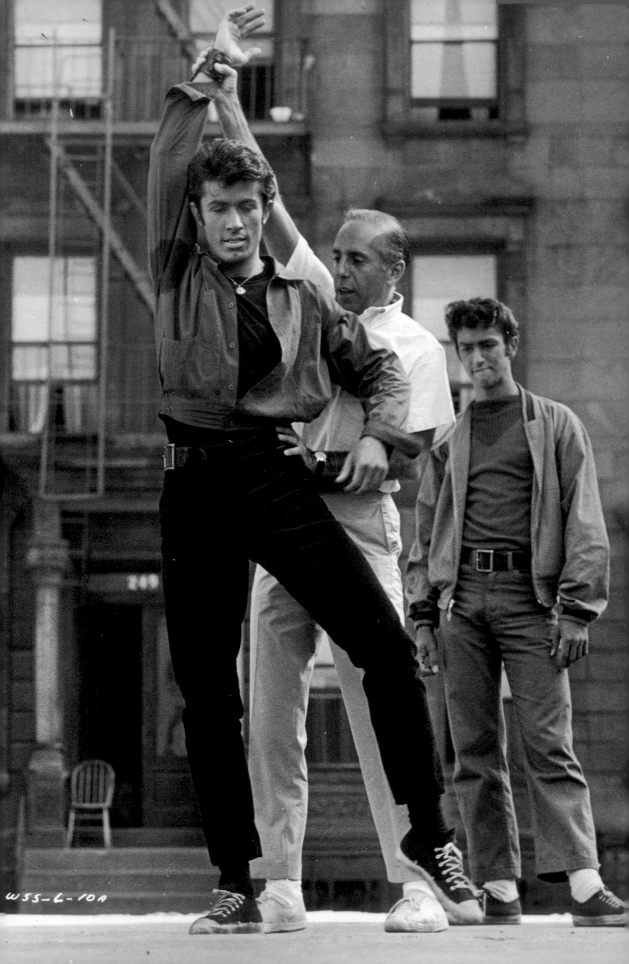

Jerome Robbins, shown here rehearsing three members of his ballet troupe for the film version of "West Side Story," is director and choreographer of Ballets: U. S. A., which opens today at the ANTA Theater. He discusses his current stage and film work with Walter Terry on Page 6.

"I found a rule for myself…which said that the higher the stakes are in a venture, the more money is involved, the more people are involved—there are corps of people you will never see who have something to do with what you're doing. Beware of that."

left. Rehearsing George Chakiris as Bernardo in film version of *West Side Story*, 1960. Eddie Verso (Juano) looks on.

above. Newspaper article on Robbins rehearsing *West Side Story*, 1960.

above. Jerome Robbins with his honorary
Oscar for Brilliant Achievements in the Art of
Choreography on Film, one of two Academy
Awards he received for *West Side Story* in
1961. He shared the Oscar for Best Director
with Robert Wise.

right. Jerome Robbins, on crane, filming *West
Side Story* on location in New York City, 1960.

Russ Tamblyn and fellow Jets in street dance scene from *West Side Story*, 1960.

"*Gypsy*...[is] a funny kind of package, like trying to wrap several watermelons into a neat bundle.... It covers a span of ten years, roams all over the country, and has the most miscellaneous cast of characters I've ever had to deal with—children of various sizes, old vaudeville actors, strippers, and all sorts of pets and stray animals. It'll be a funny show—at least, I hope so—but sad, and pretty grim, too. A kind of tragic success story, about the great American stage mother who tries to live her life through her children."

above. Jerome Robbins rehearsing with
Sandra Church in *Gypsy,* 1959. Book by Arthur
Laurents; music by Jule Styne; lyrics by
Stephen Sondheim; directed by Jerome
Robbins.

left. A newspaper clipping about *Gypsy,* 1959.

201

above. Cast of *Gypsy*, 1959.

right. Maria Karnilova, Faith Dane and
Chotzi Foley starred as the three strippers
in *Gypsy*, 1959.

Jerome Robbins (at table, obscured) meeting
with the cast of *Fiddler on the Roof*, 1964.
Robbins' former teacher Gluck-Sandor played
the role of the Rabbi in the show. Book by
Joseph Stein; music by Jerry Bock; lyrics by
Sheldon Harnick; choreography and direction
by Jerome Robbins.

"There are no dance numbers [per se] in *Fiddler*. Dance is integrated into the material of the show in a very deep way.... [What] I contributed to it was to bring it into a place where I felt... the deepest rituals of a people were enlarged to a ritual stage.... that noble thing of a race holding itself together in the face of adversity and holding on to its roots."

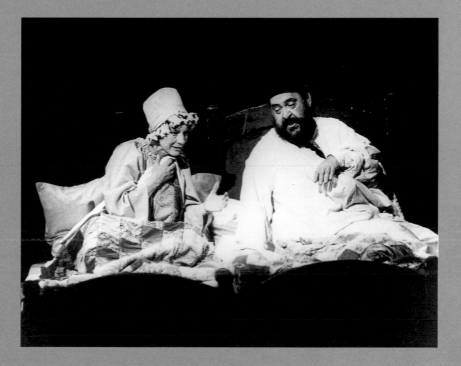

"I was born in this country.... But my parents came from that area [in Russia, near the Polish border]. I had a very emancipated, assimilated upbringing but it is curious to see how many threads of that time have woven their way down to the present day."

left. Zero Mostel as Tevye in *Fiddler on the Roof,* 1964.

above. Zero Mostel as Tevye and Maria Karnilova as Golde, 1964. That year Robbins told an interviewer from *Show Magazine* that this scene and the song "Do You Love Me?" were his favorites in the show.

"I think my Dad's greatest pleasure was *Fiddler on the Roof.* He didn't see any of the rehearsals and I invited him to the opening. He came to it and [after the performance] he came through the stage door and he saw me and he just burst into tears.

"I was so touched by it. That was one of the reasons I wanted to do that show, because of the background that I have."

left. The wedding of Tzeitel to Motel the Tailor in *Fiddler on the Roof.*

right. The Bottle dance in *Fiddler on the Roof.*

A page in Robbins' journal, watercolor, 1976.
The view is from the Bridgehampton,
Long Island, house Robbins rented several
summers in the 1970s.

6

A FERTILE NEW ERA
1965–1989

"I loved collaboration.... I always found it
stimulating and exciting and fun—and sometimes torturous. But it didn't matter. It was
always exciting to work out the problems of
the show. But then I suddenly felt it'd be nice
not to have to suit so many people, and to take
in so many people's needs, and to work just
with dancers in the simplest way. And to work
with Bach and Mozart and Stravinsky, and
out of the commercial pressure of the theater."

After *Fiddler on the Roof,* Robbins came to a rest stop after many years of forward motion. He needed a sabbatical from his usual work to recharge and decide what new paths to take. He also needed some personal time to assess changes in himself and think about what he wanted for the future.

He took no work in the commercial theater and, after *Les Noces* in 1965, didn't choreograph any new ballets in this period. But a sabbatical for him still meant working as hard as ever— just differently. In 1966, he received a National Endowment for the Arts grant to create what became The American Theatre Lab. He later described what he was doing there as experiments to see if he could "develop theatrical work as [he] would a ballet," creating the scenes organically as he went along. He said he found this project, which took the form of an unending rehearsal, the "hardest work [he'd] ever done, bar none."

No finished works came out of the two years of the Lab, but Robbins did generate material he would later incorporate into *Poppa Piece* and he told me at one point that other work he did there was not really lost but showed up in his later ballets. During this time he also studied Japanese Noh theater, and this interest was reflected later in the meditative *Watermill* (1973), which he choreographed for New York City Ballet.

Robbins also began to spend more summers at the Atlantic Ocean. He always had a great need to be near water, soothing as it was to his hyperactive nervous system. He began renting for a month at a time in the Hamptons on Long Island, and that is where we met. Only at the beach could he truly relax and rest. He'd go to the beach in the late morning, bringing a rubber raft for the occasional swim, a little lunch, some reading, sometimes a backgammon board, and he could sit for hours. Robbins loved "found" objects and one day discovered the perfect flat board and heavy stick on the beach, which he turned into a backrest. At the end of the day, he'd bury the wood pieces, and then uncover them his next time in the sun.

In later years, he bought a small 1930s oceanfront cottage on Dune Road in Bridgehampton, Long Island, and shared it with his dogs Nick, a gray-black terrier mix, Annie, an abused dog

A page in Robbins' journal, 1976. Beach fence.

Monday Aug 16 – Beach.

I'm writing more – + liking it. Such associative memories arise. I'm not afraid of it at this point. Don't know when it will stop or where it will go.

Sunshine today. Finally. Weekend with Dilli, Adam + fog + rain. Nice – but damp. Now sand + here + I've written for about an hr!!

Aug 18th. 76.

found on the subway in New York City, and later, Tess, another mutt. If it was lucky to be one of Robbins' cherished friends, to be one of his cherished dogs was luckier still: their special diet meals were cooked daily by the maestro himself.

In 1968, after not working at New York City Ballet for eight years, Robbins was asked to do a small piece for an upcoming gala. This casual invitation led to his choreographing *Dances at a Gathering* (1969), which began a fertile new era of work, all almost exclusively with the New York City Ballet.

The Goldberg Variations (1971), staged to Bach's glorious music, became one of Robbins' most critically acclaimed ballets and was one of his personal favorites as well. All through the 1970s and '80s, he worked with great energy at New York City Ballet, producing over forty original ballets.

By the mid-1980s, Robbins began to worry that many of his Broadway works would be lost forever. Ballets dropped out of sight, of course, but at least most he considered important were being performed by New York City Ballet and in the repertoires of other companies worldwide. What began as a library preservation project ultimately turned into the celebratory *Jerome Robbins' Broadway* (1989), where the best of his Broadway work was staged for a new generation of viewers and preserved on tape for future generations beyond.

left. Robbins and I, in front of his beach
cottage in Bridgehampton, Long Island, 1984.
He kept the place simple and "beachy,"
making only minor changes over the years—
adding a small guest bedroom and, much later,
a lap pool.

above. Jerome Robbins and myself in
Bridgehampton, 1984.

A Silver Lining

Man Finds Dog! breathed balletomanes with relief last week as the end of the great Manhattan doghunt slowly transpired throughout the New York State Theater. Nick was back and Jerome Robbins had him. Since June 15, when Nick, a terrier-like mongrel, disappeared from outside a store on East 83rd Street, the choreographer had hunted high and low, inserted handbills in ballet programs, postered the theater and as much of New York as he could, appealed on television. and placed ads in the newspapers. At last Mr. Robbins, while. on a personal expedition, saw Nick near 49th Street and Ninth Avenue in the custody of a man said to be locally well known. "I swapped some dough for the dog, he gave me the dog and split," Mr. Robbins said. After recovering Nick, Mr. Robbins said, he received some 40 phone calls from others who were sure they too had found him.

left. Robbins and myself at a New York City Ballet gala, 1974.

above. Happy ending to search for Nick, Robbins' much beloved dog, the *New York Times,* July 2, 1978.

"It was a shocking change. From nothing to—to everything. And I wasn't prepared for it. I think really what happened, when I think back on it, now, was that somewhere in my early life I...thought that all my career and personal problems would change once I was a success. Well, here I was a success and although there was much more opportunity and attention, none of my personal problems changed. I realized I had to look somewhere else rather than to being well known and accomplished, to straighten out inside of myself."

Jerome Robbins often made his own calendars. He pasted this one for October 1973 into his journal.

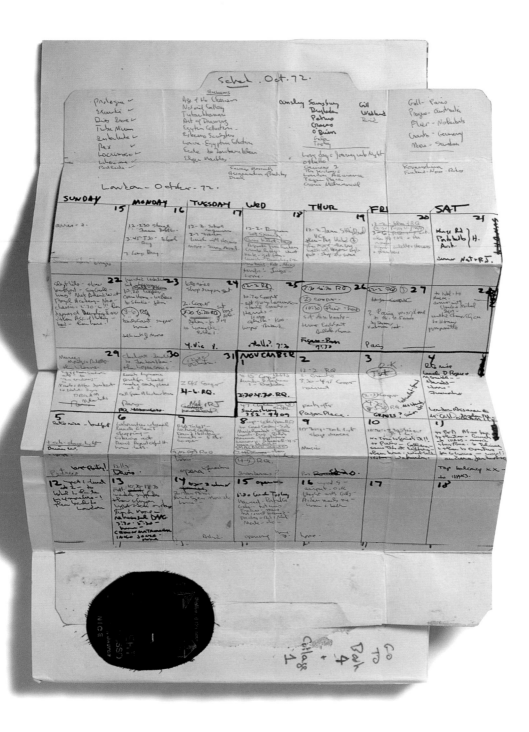

above. Journal page, Italy, 1973.

right. Journal page, Israel, 1977.

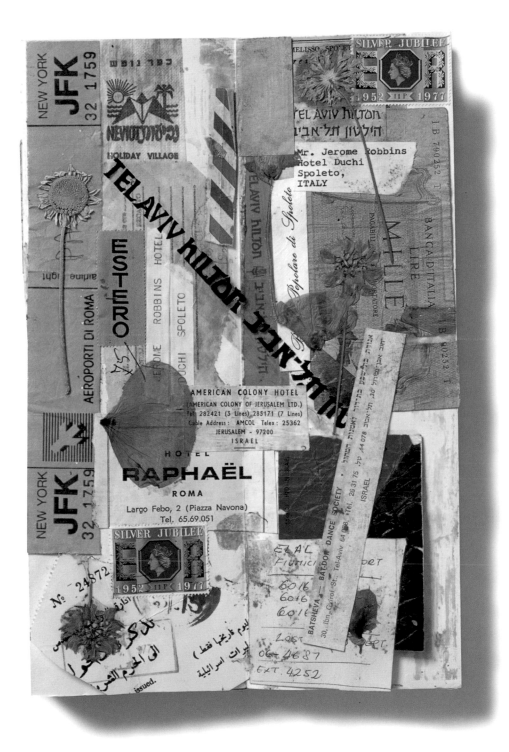

"The possibilities of the human body are endless. Why not use them all? Why limit ourselves to a set language which in spite of its good qualities is no longer fit to express the feelings and problems of today?"

left. Journal cover, 1974.

above. Half of a page in Robbins' journal, Paris, 1977.

above. Journal cover, 1973.

right. Journal page, pressed flowers, 1973.

"I did not make any decision to quit
  Broadway. I just started to work
  again in ballet and continued
  to work in ballet. There was just
  nothing in the theater that
  interested me enough...at the time.
  I was offered some shows—but
  there were very few in the 25 years
  that I wasn't working on Broadway
  that I wish I had gotten a lick at.
    "Music changed. What is
  popular on radio, discs, television,
  is not what was popular prior to
  1965. There are fascinating things
  in the rock revolution, but I don't
  know how many memorable scores
  they make for musical comedies
  as they used to make them."

Jerome Robbins rehearsing Elaine May in
The Office, written by Irene Maria Fornes, 1967.
The play never opened because Robbins,
dissatisfied with the production, closed it
before opening night.

The American Ballet Theatre production of
Les Noces, music by Igor Stravinsky, choreo-
graphed for American Ballet Theatre, 1965.
Principal dancer, Erin Martin.

Oct 23

Balanchine teaches — + how he teaches — he doesn't "give a class — its not just a warm up + work out for the dancers — It is a master class in how to do + he insists each particular moment of classic + basic ballet vocabulary with + how + why + + a detail of such elevated elegance + perfection. If I am known as a perfectionist one should attend his classes. Unfortunately, one can see the attitude of the dancers still remains aloof + apart —— "that crazy man" — they don't heart do + cut if he insists on a detail (each of which is basic + never ornamental) they hold it for a few passes + then drop it. What a revelation the classes are. "Each step, each movement must be a miracle" — apropos of port de bras — "Breath your steps — "There is no sex (no difference of the sexes) in ballet. I'm going to film it all as soon as possible.

JUNGLE EXPRESS

Oct. 24.
Changes — or just agits?
O.K. Indecisions — commitments to Royal — what — which Ravel — which program notes — which corrals for scherzo —

Oct 25th — "L'Enfant" — Ravel — with sans — see Seth

above. Journal page, 1974.

right. Jerome Robbins and George Balanchine backstage at New York City Ballet's Stravinsky Festival, 1972.

"*Dances at a Gathering* [in 1969] is about my
life in that period—just a feeling of love and
relationships with people."

Robbins rehearsing Allegra Kent in *Dances at a Gathering*, 1969, regarded as one of his masterworks.

Patricia McBride and Edward Villella in *pas de deux* from New York City Ballet production of *Dances at a Gathering*, 1969.

"[Stopping by the New York City Ballet office
one day, I was asked if I wanted to choreograph
something for an upcoming gala.] I had
rehearsed Eddie Villella and Patty McBride in
Faun and I was so impressed by them that
I said, 'Well, I'll do a pas de deux for them to
Chopin music (which I love) and I don't know
which pieces, but, yes, I think I'll do a pas de
deux.... And that was the beginning."

"I worked to a point where they couldn't attend the next rehearsal, so I asked for two other dancers, and then I asked for two more dancers, and then I thought, 'Well, six is going to be the most it gets to.' And I got up to I don't know how many, and then I showed it to Balanchine."

"And [Balanchine] looked at it and…he said, 'More, more. You gotta make it like popcorn. Keep eating, keep eating. You gotta do more…'"

Multiple exposure of Violet Verdy in *Dances at a Gathering*, 1969.

"[Balanchine] came backstage after the opening
and this is one of the rare experiences I had in
my life, which is, he came to the stage door and
he looked at me and he put his arms around
me and gave me the Russian kisses and looked
me in the eye and no other comment.... I was
so touched by that."

left. Multiple exposure of cast of dancers in finale of *Dances at a Gathering*.

above. Curtain call for Jerome Robbins and company, *Dances at a Gathering*, 1969.

"*Watermill*...was a healing period. What I
was healing from I don't know. It was a
re-evaluation.... I said [to Balanchine] that
it's going to be the opposite of the kind of
ballets I've been doing as far as the dancing is
concerned. It's going to be a search into
another place. George said that it's a ballet
about there being no time. And that was when
he made a remark to me about choreographers
—that we dare to get our fingertips into the
land where there are no names for anything."

above. Jerome Robbins rehearsing Edward
Villella in the New York City Ballet production
of *Watermill,* 1972. This meditative ballet
was controversial with critics, some of whom
bemoaned the absence of dance.

left. Edward Villella, Jerome Robbins and
Hermes Conde (rear) rehearsing *Watermill,*
1972.

Edward Villella in *Watermill*, 1972.

left. Helgi Tomasson in the New York City
Ballet production of *Dybbuk*, 1974.

above. Gelsey Kirkland and Bart Cook in
Dybbuk.

above left. Jerome Robbins and Leonard
Bernstein taking a bow on opening night of
Dybbuk, May 19, 1974. Robbins, in an interview,
said that while he wanted "a very hard
diamond of a ballet," he felt Bernstein wanted
"a big dramatic" thing. They never quite
got in sync and Robbins was not completely
satisfied with the ballet.

above right. Robbins and I, opening night of
Dybbuk, 1974.

right. Robbins and George Balanchine link
arms, *Pulcinella,* 1972.

Robbins rehearsing Mikhail Baryshnikov in *Other Dances*, 1976.

Suzanne Farrell and Peter Martins in New York
City Ballet production of *Concerto in G*, 1975.

"If I don't care about every minute of a ballet, it is not going to be as good as if I do."

"[Alban] Berg wrote this piece [the score I chose for *In Memory Of...*] to honor a young girl, the daughter of friends of his, who died of polio. But so much else was incorporated into that score, of his own biography.... It was written in 1935 [and] he was slowly being stripped of his homeland [Germany]. He also was very ill himself... All of this within the structure of twelve-tone serial music.

"At the same time, he was a wonderful dramatic and lyric writer. He never lost a sense of the emotion he was going to portray. Too many people have passed on in recent years. I think, finally, [the ballet] should not be connected to one person but to the sense of losing people, and the struggles that they go through when they're ill, and die. And hopefully, arrive at a peace for themselves. The quote at the end of the Berg, from the prophet Elijah, is: 'It is enough. It is enough. Take me. I'm ready to go. And I leave gratefully this world and enter the other world.'"

Suzanne Farrell and Adam Lüders in the
New York City Ballet production of *In Memory
Of...*, 1985.

"I rebel violently...against being classified and being specific about what my ballets are about. Try to ask a painter what he thought about when he put red in one spot and blue in another. I work for months, days and hours and keep changing until many, many moments come from a deep unconscious stream. Then I work through layers until I get to the level I call the key or spine of that work. Once I hit that, the work pours forth. Before that I change, alter, probe, discard and examine. So you can see that by the time I get to it, I'm hard put to analyze all the stages I've gone through to get there."

A duet performed by Fred Astaire and Rita Hayworth in the 1942 musical *You Were Never Lovelier* inspired Robbins' ballet, *I'm Old Fashioned,* danced by New York City Ballet in 1983. Robbins and Balanchine were both great admirers of Fred Astaire.

Glass Pieces, with music by Philip Glass, 1983, juxtaposed a coolly elegant classicism against Glass' minimalist score. The set design is credited as a collaboration of Jerome Robbins and Ronald Bates.

The New York City Ballet in *Antique Epigraphs* (1984), set to Claude Debussy's *Six Epigraphes Antiques* and *Syrinx*, conjures up images of friezes from ancient Greece.

"I've been thinking about my Broadway shows. I love those works, and I really didn't want them just to become legends and disappear. I wanted to put those Broadway numbers back on the stage and record them, and, after that, have them there as a document of the work I've done in the musical theater. Ballets, if good, become part of a repertory and are constantly performed by a large number of ballet companies. Shows run and then stop.... I liked what I did and I liked the results of working with all those collaborators, and I just don't want to lose those works."

left. Rehearsing *Jerome Robbins' Broadway,* 1989. The T-shirt is a gag gift from the cast.

above top. Rehearsing the Bathing Beauties ballet from *High Button Shoes* for *Jerome Robbins' Broadway,* 1989.

above. Rehearsing the Mack Sennett ballet from *High Button Shoes* for *Jerome Robbins' Broadway,* 1989. Assisting on the production is dancer Grover Dale (walking in plaid shirt), who was in the original 1957 production of *West Side Story.*

The full cast in *Jerome Robbins' Broadway*, which premiered on February 26, 1989.

Jerome Robbins at his desk in Bridgehampton,
Long Island, New York, November 1988.

7 LAST BOWS
1990–1998

"It's got to be something in which the creative part of me will be satisfied.... Some things are offered to me, and I think: 'That's going to tire me. But it's not going to try me.'"

In 1990, Robbins felt he needed a break from his responsibilities as Co-Balletmaster in Chief with Peter Martins at New York City Ballet. They'd shared this title after Balanchine's death in 1983, and now Robbins took a leave of absence from his duties. Although he was healthy and vigorous, he was nonetheless tired from the long period of work on the retrospective of his Broadway shows.

His thoughts turned increasingly to the project that came to be called *Poppa Piece.* He had begun working on it more intermittently in the early 1970s, with short handwritten sketches on yellow pads, mostly during summers at his beach house. He once acknowledged to me that just working on it was therapeutic for him and a helpful tool when his agitated thoughts became hard to manage. The name of the piece shifted over the years— at one time it was called *Rabinowitz on Rabinowitz*—and was at first only casually referred to as his Poppa piece.

Poppa Piece would evolve into a highly theatrical, autobiographical dance-drama—it's form unique to Robbins' creative abilities. In it, he tried to dramatize the trajectory of his struggles with his father and manhood, his Jewishness and his searing experiences at the hands of the House Un-American Activities Committee (HUAC). Not surprisingly, he had set an extremely difficult task for himself, pushing his own limits and the limits of form. By the mid-1980s, he alternated between great resolve to mount the piece and the agonizing wish to abandon it altogether.

In 1991, Robbins began a workshop production of *Poppa Piece* at Lincoln Center. Those who participated were amazed by his willingness to work with such painful personal material. Rehearsal videos reveal that what he did manage to stage was emotionally and dramatically powerful. In particular, a ballet with dancers on bicycles was as beautiful as any of the "object" ballets he created in his younger years. But he seemed to hit a wall each time he approached the HUAC material and, whatever the full reason, Robbins withdrew the piece without finishing it.

But he didn't stop working. Choreographing again at the New York City Ballet, Robbins created *2 & 3 Part Inventions* (1994) with young dancers from the School of American Ballet and then *West Side Story Suite* (1995) and *Brandenberg* (1997) for the company. Pressing urgently at the back of his mind was *Les Noces,* originally staged for American Ballet Theatre in 1965. Robbins was determined that it become a presence in the New York City Ballet repertoire as well.

Portrait of Robbins' desk with glasses,
Bridgehampton, November 1992.

He began restaging the ballet in December of 1997 and continued on into May of 1998. *Les Noces,* which means "The Wedding," is a dance cantata based on a Russian peasant wedding and is extremely difficult to stage. The music is complicated and dense; the dancers must count continuously. And the monolithic score is just one layer of many: richly elaborate costumes, multiple props, numerous entrances and exits.

It was a daunting task even for someone perfectly fit, and Robbins' health was extremely precarious. In 1994, he'd had an operation to repair a heart valve. Now his balance was impaired due to a form of Parkinson's, and his short term memory was becoming increasingly problematic. He had the kind of problems that would keep most of us from leaving the house, let alone heading to Lincoln Center every day for intense rehearsals in a high-pressured atmosphere. The courage required to work under those conditions was breathtaking. His only seeming concession to being hampered by his health was a decision to use taped music instead of the twelve choral singers and full orchestra. This kind of "corner cutting" would have been unthinkable in earlier years.

When Robbins came out at the curtain on opening night to take bow after bow to extravagant applause, he looked frail and walked haltingly, his skin translucent as parchment. Though no one in the audience could fail to see his obvious fatigue and weak state, few knew just how fearsome an effort of will was required of him to mount this ballet.

The day after *Les Noces* opened, Robbins collapsed from the strain and was hospitalized for two weeks. When I talked to him from London on his release, he was still very fragile and had difficulty describing where he was—in the city? at the beach house?—but he was very affectionate and kept asking me when I would be getting to New York. In retrospect, I think he was telling me he was afraid he might never see me again. A month later, Jerry suffered a massive stroke and was dead, two months short of his eightieth birthday. I never did see him again, but in my heart, he speaks to me every day.

Jerome Robbins on deck of Bridgehampton house with, from left, Nick and Annie, early 1980s.

Jerome Robbins rehearsing Mikhail
Baryshnikov for the White Oak Dance Project
debut of *A Suite of Dances* in New York
City, March 1994.

Mikhail Baryshnikov in a dress rehearsal of *A Suite of Dances*, 1994.

Wendy Whelan and Peter Boal in
Brandenberg, 1997.

Collage for *Poppa Piece*, late 1970s. Robbins
created this collage and placed it on an easel in
the office at his house in New York City while he
worked on the project.

New York City Ballet rehearsal of revival of *Les Noces,* 1998. Assisting Robbins are, to his immediately left, Jean Pierre Frohlich, Ballet Master at New York City Ballet, and James Moore (further left), a former Ballet Master at American Ballet Theatre who assisted on the first production of *Les Noces* in 1965 and who continues to stage this ballet for companies all over the world.

left. Alexandra Ansanelli and Robert
Wersinger in *Les Noces*, 1998.

above. Christopher Wheeldon and Sébastien
Marcovici in *Les Noces*, 1998.

Alexandra Ansanelli and company in
Les Noces, 1998.

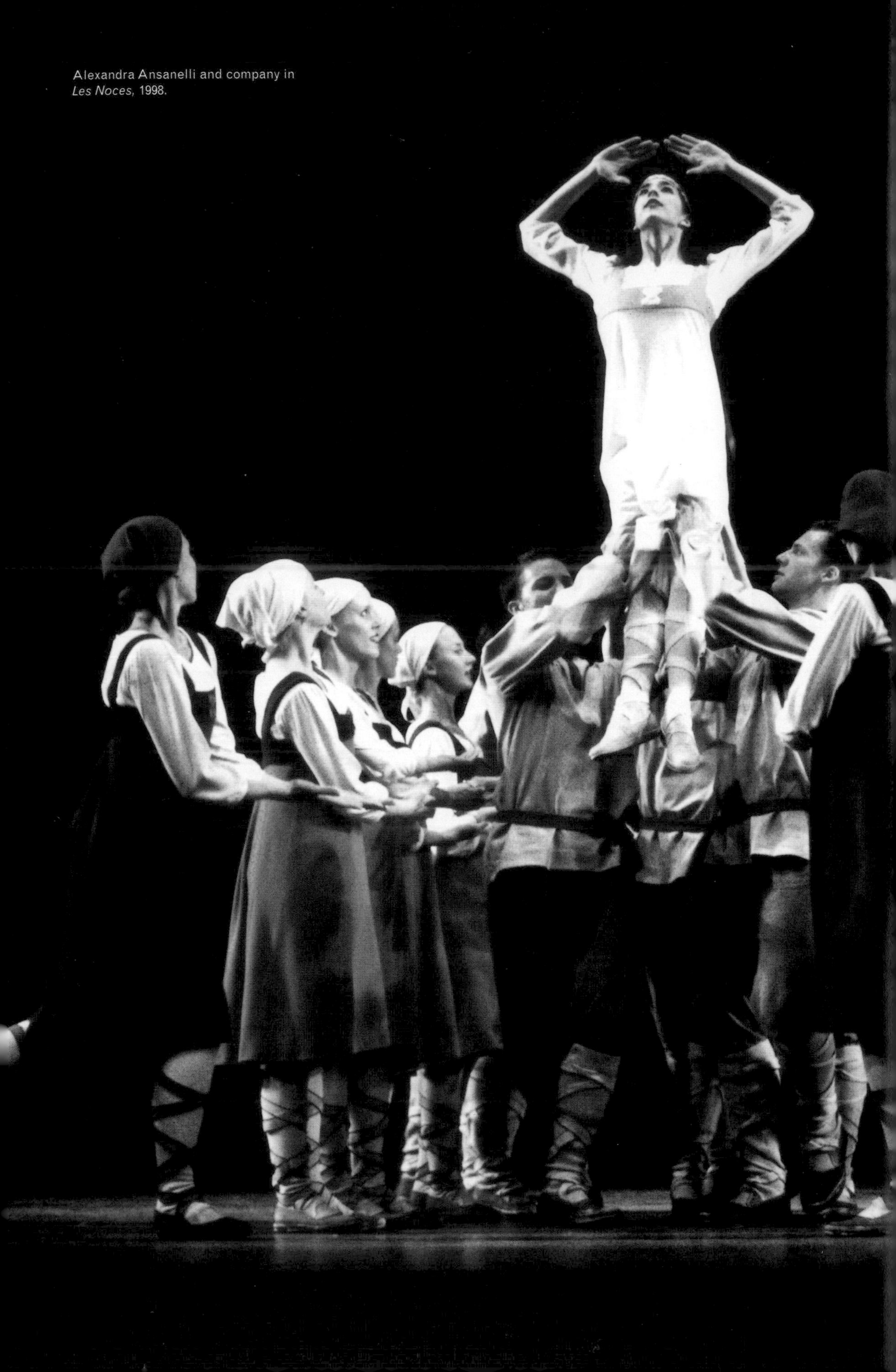

Journal page, 1978. This collage includes a
photograph of Leo Tolstoy in his eighties,
sitting in a chair. Robbins was fascinated by
Tolstoy and read biographies of the author
and all of his works.

"[Watching a ballet performance] reminds people much too poignantly of their own mortality. So they say, 'Books are better— or paintings or sculptures—because they can be touched. Because they will last."

"Ballet makes me feel like an author. I can say whatever I want to say, limited only by my own capacities and those of my dancers."

Robbins taking a bow.

AWARDS

c.1946	Donaldson Award *Billion Dollar Baby*
1947	Antoinette Perry (Tony) Award for Best Choreographer *High Button Shoes*
1947	Donaldson Award *High Button Shoes*
1948	New York Drama Critics Award *High Button Shoes*
1948	New York Drama Critics Award *High Button Shoes*
1950	*Dance Magazine* Award for Outstanding Achievement
1951	Donaldson Award *The King and I*
1952	Donaldson Award *Two's Company*
1953	Sylvania Award "Ford 50th Anniversary Show"
1954	Donaldson Award *The Pajama Game*
1955	Emmy Award for Best Choreographer "Peter Pan" (televised)
1956	*Look Magazine* Award "Peter Pan" (televised)
1956	Box Office Blue Ribbon Award *The King and I* (film)
1957	*Dance Magazine* Award for Outstanding Achievement
1958	Antoinette Perry (Tony) Award for Best Choreographer *West Side Story* (musical)
1958	London Evening Standard Drama Award (England) *West Side Story* (musical)
1959	City of New York Citation bestowed by Mayor Wagner *Ballets U.S.A.*
1959	Theatre Des Nations Award named Best Choreographer
1961	Academy of Motion Picture Arts and Sciences Award (Oscar) Best Director: *West Side Story* (with Robert Wise) Honorary Award for Brilliant Achievements in the Art of Choreography on Film

1961	Writers' Guild of America West: Laurel Award
	West Side Story (film)
1961	SBI Gold Owl Award for Best Choreography
	West Side Story (film)
1961	Screen Directors Guild Award
	West Side Story (film)
1964	Chevalier de l'Ordre des Arts et des Lettres (France)
1965	Antoinette Perry (Tony) Award for Best Director
	Antoinette Perry (Tony) Award for Best Choreographer
	Fiddler on the Roof (stage)
1965	Drama Critics Award for Best Musical
	Fiddler on the Roof (stage)
1966	National Endowment for the Arts grant
1967	Brandeis University, Waltham, Massachusetts:
	Creative Arts Award for Theater
1971	City of Paris Award for Best Ballet (France)
	Les Noces in International Dance Festival
1974	Ohio University, Athens, Ohio: Honorary Degree
	of Doctor of Humane Letters
1976	Handel Medallion, City of New York
1976	Capezio Dance Award
1979	America-Israel Arts, Sciences and Humanities Award
1979	Theater Hall of Fame (New York)
1980	City University of New York: Honorary Doctorate
1981	Washington, DC: Kennedy Center Honors Award
1982	America-Israel Cultural Foundation's King Solomon Award
	for Artistic Achievement
1984	Brandeis University, Waltham, Massachusetts:
	Creative Arts Award for Dance
1985	American Academy of Arts and Letters:
	American Honorary Member
1985	New York University, New York, New York: Honorary Doctor of Fine Arts
1985	The Anglo-American Contemporary Dance Foundation:
	Fred Astaire Award for Lifetime Achievement in Dance
1988	Royal Danish Theatre, Denmark: Hans Christian Andersen
	Ballet Award
1988	National Endowment for the Arts: National Medal of Arts Award
1989	Antoinette Perry (Tony) Award for Best Director of a Musical
	Jerome Robbins' Broadway
1990	Bank of Delaware: Commonwealth Award of Distinguished
	Service in the Dramatic Arts
1990	Commandeur de l'Ordre des Arts et des Lettres (France)
1993	Chevalier dans l'Ordre National de la Legion d'Honneur (France)
1993	Fellow of the American Academy of Arts and Sciences
1997	Governor's Arts Award (New York)

LIST OF WORKS

EARLY PERFORMANCE AND CHOREOGRAPHY

1936–1938	Gluck-Sandor & Felicia Sorel's The Dance Center	Appeared in studio performances.
1937–1941	Camp Tamiment	Weekly revues. Appeared under name of Jerry Robyns (1937-1940) and as Jerome Robbins (1941).
1937	*The Brothers Ashkenazi*	Yiddish Art Theatre. First speaking role (one line in Yiddish).
1938	*Great Lady*	Performed in chorus of Broadway musical.
1939	"Death of a Loyalist"	Danced role of the Prisoner in this piece, his first credited choreography (as Jerry Robyns), in Camp Tamiment revue, *Shooting Stars.*
1939	*Stars in Your Eyes*	Performed in chorus of Broadway musical.
1939	*Straw Hat Revue*	First uncredited choreography for Broadway. Revue was developed at Camp Tamiment, where Robbins choreographed the number, "Piano and Lute," which appeared in the Broadway version (with Robbins dancing in it). Credit for the entire show's choreography on Broadway was given to Jerome Andrews.
1939	*Keep Off the Grass*	Performed in chorus of Broadway show.
1940–1949	Ballet Theatre	Performed in the corps until 1941, when he was made soloist. Originated roles in *Three Virgins and a Devil* (the Youth; 1941), *Helen of Troy* (Hermes; 1942), *Romeo and Juliet* (Benvolio; 1943) and many other works, including his own ballets.
1949	New York City Ballet	Joined company and performed leading roles in his own works and those of George Balanchine, including *Bourrée Fantasque* (1949), *Prodigal Son* (1950) and *Tyl Ulenspiegel* (1951). Became Associate Artistic Director his second year. Stopped performing regularly in the early 1950s. In later years he occasionally took a role as in *Pulcinella, Circus Polka* and as Drosselmeyer in *The Nutcracker.*

BALLETS

1944	*Fancy Free** (Leonard Bernstein, composer)	Ballet Theatre
1945	*Interplay** (Morton Gould, composer)	Billy Rose's Concert Varieties, the Ziegfield Theater
1946	*Afterthought* (Igor Stravinsky, composer)	American Society for Russian Relief
1946	*Facsimile** (Leonard Bernstein, composer)	Ballet Theatre
1947	*Summer Day** (Sergei Prokofiev, composer)	Ballet Theatre

1947	*Pas de Trois* (Hector Berlioz, composer)	Colonel Basil's Ballet Russe de Monte Carlo
1949	*The Guests** (Marc Blitzstein, composer)	New York City Ballet
1950	*Jones Beach** with George Balanchine (Juriaan Andriessen, composer)	New York City Ballet
1950	*Age of Anxiety** based on poem by W.H. Auden (Leonard Bernstein, composer)	New York City Ballet
1951	*The Cage* (Igor Stravinsky, composer)	New York City Ballet
1951	*Pied Piper* (Aaron Copland, composer)	New York City Ballet
1952	*Ballade* (Claude Debussy, composer)	New York City Ballet
1953	*Afternoon of a Faun* (Claude Debussy, composer)	New York City Ballet
1953	*Fanfare* (Benjamin Britten, composer)	New York City Ballet
1954	*Quartet* (Sergei Prokofiev, composer)	New York City Ballet
1956	*The Concert (Or, the Perils of Everybody)* (Frederic Chopin, composer)	New York City Ballet
1958	*New York Export: Opus Jazz* (Robert Prince, composer)	Ballets U.S.A., premiere at Festival of Two Worlds, Spoleto, Italy
1959	*Moves* (silent)	Ballets U.S.A., premiere at Festival of Two Worlds, Spoleto, Italy. U.S. State Department Tour.
1961	*3 X 3* (Georges Auric, composer)	Ballets U.S.A., premiere at Spoleto Festival, Italy
1961	*Events* (Robert Prince, composer)	Ballets U.S.A., premiere at Spoleto Festival, Italy
1965	*Les Noces* (Igor Stravinsky, composer)	American Ballet Theatre (name formerly changed on first performance in Belgrade, Yugoslavia, September 5, 1956)
1969	*Dances at a Gathering* (Frederic Chopin, composer)	New York City Ballet
1970	*In the Night* (Frederic Chopin, composer)	New York City Ballet
1970	*The Firebird* with George Balanchine (Igor Stravinsky, composer)	New York City Ballet
1971	*The Goldberg Variations* (Johann Sebastian Bach, composer)	New York City Ballet
1972	*Watermill* (Teiji Ito, composer)	New York City Ballet
1972	*Scherzo Fantastique* (Igor Stravinsky, composer)	New York City Ballet, Stravinsky Festival
1972	*Circus Polka** (Igor Stravinsky, composer)	New York City Ballet, Stravinsky Festival

1972	*Dumbarton Oaks* (Igor Stravinsky, composer)	New York City Ballet, Stravinsky Festival
1972	*Pulcinella** with George Balanchine (Igor Stravinsky, composer)	New York City Ballet, Stravinsky Festival
1972	*Requiem Canticles* (Igor Stravinsky, composer)	New York City Ballet, Stravinsky Festival
1973	*Beethoven Pas de Deux* (Ludvig van Beethoven, composer) renamed *Four Bagatelles* in 1974	New York City Ballet
1973	*An Evening's Waltzes* (Sergei Prokofiev, composer)	New York City Ballet
1973	*Celebration: The Art of the Pas de Deux* (various composers)	Spoleto Festival, Italy. Danced by 5 couples representing different nations, dedicated to memory of choreographer John Cranko.
1974	*Dybbuk* (Leonard Bernstein, composer) renamed *Dybbuk Variations* in 1974; *Suite of Dances* in 1980	New York City Ballet
1975	*Concerto in G* (Maurice Ravel, composer) renamed *In G Major* in 1975	New York City Ballet, Ravel Festival
1975	*Introduction and Allegro for Harp* (Maurice Ravel, composer)	New York City Ballet, Ravel Festival
1975	*Ma Mere l'Oye* (Maurice Ravel, composer) later renamed *Mother Goose*	New York City Ballet, Ravel Festival
1975	*Une Barque sur l'Ocean* (Maurice Ravel, composer)	New York City Ballet, Ravel Festival
1975	*Chansons Madecasses* (Maurice Ravel, composer)	New York City Ballet, Ravel Festival
1976	*Other Dances* (Frederic Chopin, composer)	Star Spangled Gala for the Library of the Performing Arts
1978	*Tricolore* with Peter Martins and Jean-Pierre Bonnefous (Georges Auric, composer)	New York City Ballet. A dance in 3 sections; Robbins choreographed third section, "Marche de la Garde Republicane."
1978	*A Sketch Book* with Peter Martins, works-in-progress (George Frideric Handel, Heinrich Biber, Gioacchino [Antonio] Rossini, Georg Philipp Telemann, Guiseppe Verdi, composers)	New York City Ballet. Contained elements of "projected" (unfinished) ballet, *The Arts of the Gentleman.*
1979	*The Four Seasons* (Guiseppe Verdi, composer)	New York City Ballet
1979	*Le Bourgeois Gentilhomme* with George Balanchine based on play by Jean-Baptiste Moliere (Richard Strauss and Jean-Baptiste Lully, composers)	New York City Ballet
1979	*Opus 19/The Dreamer* (Sergei Prokofiev, composer)	New York City Ballet

1981	*Rondo* (Wolfgang Amadeus Mozart, composer)	New York City Ballet
1981	*Andantino* (Piotr Ilich Tchaikovsky, composer)	New York City Ballet, Tchaikovsky Festival
1981	*Valse à Cinq Temps* (Piotr Ilich Tchaikovsky, composer)	New York City Ballet, Tchaikovsky Festival. A dance with sections by several choreographers; Robbins did fourth section, "Tempo di Valse."
1981	*Piano Pieces* (Piotr Ilich Tchaikovsky, composer)	New York City Ballet, Tchaikovsky Festival
1981	*Allegro con Grazia* (Piotr Ilich Tchaikovsky, composer)	New York City Ballet, Tchaikovsky Festival
1981	Jerome Robbins Chamber Dance Company	Tour of the People's Republic of China, sponsored by the US International Communications Agency
1982	*Gershwin Concerto* (George Gershwin, composer)	New York City Ballet
1982	*Concertino* (Igor Stravinsky, composer)	New York City Ballet
1982	*Four Chamber Works* (Igor Stravinsky, composer)	New York City Ballet, Stravinsky Centennial Celebration
1983	*Glass Pieces* (Phillp Glass, composer)	New York City Ballet
1983	*I'm Old Fashioned* (Morton Gould, composer, based on a theme by Jerome Kern)	New York City Ballet
1984	*Antique Epigraphs* (Claude Debussy, composer)	New York City Ballet
1984	*Brahms/Handel* with Twyla Tharp (Johannes Brahms, composer, based on a theme by George Frideric Handel)	New York City Ballet
1985	*Eight Lines* (Steve Reich, composer)	New York City Ballet
1985	*In Memory Of...* (Alban Berg, composer)	New York City Ballet
1986	*Quiet City* (Aaron Copland, composer)	New York City Ballet
1986	*Piccolo Balletto* (Igor Stravinsky, composer)	New York City Ballet
1988	*Ives, Songs* (Charles Ives, composer)	New York City Ballet
1994	*A Suite of Dances* (Johann Sebastian Bach, composer)	White Oak Project with Mikhail Baryshnikov
1994	*2 & 3 Part Inventions* (Johann Sebastian Bach, composer)	School of American Ballet
1995	*West Side Story Suite* (Leonard Bernstein, composer)	New York City Ballet
1997	*Brandenburg* (Johann Sebastian Bach, composer)	New York City Ballet

* Indicates ballets in which Robbins danced also.

SOURCE NOTES

INTRODUCTION

p. 9: *"...I'm a choreographer."*: Deborah Jowitt, "Back, again, to ballet," *The New York Times Magazine,* 8 December 1974, p. 109.

p. 13: *always playing jokes.*: Donald Saddler, conversation with author, New York City, 28 January 2000.

p. 13: *"...wicked sense of humor"*: Tanaquil Le Clercq, interview with Rick Whitaker, *Ballet Review,* Summer 1998, p. 18.

p. 13: *always full of mischief.*: Tanaquil Le Clercq, telephone conversation with author, 23 March 2000.

p. 14: *"...the most prepared people"*: Hal Prince, *Contradictions: Notes on Twenty-Six Years in the Theatre* (New York: Dodd, Mead & Co., 1974), p. 32.

p. 14: *her part in* The Cage*.*: Robert Sabin, "The Creative Evolution of *The Cage,*" *Dance Magazine,* August 1955, p. 59.

p. 15: *"Your Assistant, Abbott."*: Eleanor Roberts, "Ballet Brings Fame to Ex-Chorus Boy," *Boston Post Magazine,* 8 May 1948, p. 4.

p. 16: *years they worked together.*: Marilyn Hunt, "Robbins Speaks!," *Dance Magazine,* September 1997, p. 40.

p. 19: *threatened with exposure relating to his sexual life*: Amanda Vaill, conversation with author, 10 January 2000.

p. 19: *... with great energy and focus.*: T. Le Clercq, telephone conversation with author, 23 March 2000.

p. 21: *"...out of this book?"*: Fay Greenbaum, conversation with author, New York City, 21 February 2000.

I. BEGINNINGS:
THE MAKING OF AN ARTIST 1918–1939

p. 23: *"...opened up, waiting..."*: Robert Kotlowitz, "Corsets, Corned Beef and Choreography," *Show: The Magazine of the Arts,* December 1964, p. 39.

p. 24: *"...could rule the world."*: Sonia Cullinen, telephone conversation with author, 21 August 2000.

p. 24: *"...the way they were."*: R. Kotlowitz, *Show: The Magazine of the Arts,* December 1964, p. 38.

p. 27: *"...plunged into it."*: Emily Coleman, "From Tutus to T-Shirts," *The New York Times Magazine,* 8 October 1961, pp. 30, 32.

p. 27: *"...a way we liked."*: Mervyn Rothstein, "Jerome Robbins Dances Back to Broadway," *The New York Times,* 19 February 1989, sect. 2, p. 15.

p. 37: *"...my father's [corset] business..."*: Article in *Concert Varieties* program, June 1945.

p. 38: *"...garage on 54th Street."*: Jerome Robbins, interview with Clive Barnes, New York City, 1973.

p. 41: *"...to do something bigger."*: "Bringing Back Robbins's 'Fancy'": Tobi Tobias interview in *Dance Magazine,* January 1980, p. 69.

p. 42: *his sister and Alyce Bentley.*: Anna Kisselgoff, "Jerome Robbins, 79, Is Dead: Giant of Ballet and Broadway," *The New York Times,* 30 July 1998, p. 1.

p. 42: *"'...while you're still growing.'"*: Jerome Robbins, interview with Ellen Sorrin, audiotape made for Oral History Project, Dance Collection, Library of the Performing Arts at Lincoln Center, New York City, 28 November 1995. In interviews, Robbins sometimes referred to his teacher Gluck-Sandor as simply "Sandor." For the sake of clarity, he is referred to as Gluck-Sandor throughout these quotes.

p. 42: *"...used it very deeply."*: Ibid.

p. 45: *"...everything he did."*: Ibid.

p. 46: *"...you'd be all right.'"*: Ibid.

p. 48: *"...they made it $15."*: Alan M. Kriegsman, "Jerome Robbins at 60: Some Vital Reflections," *The Los Angeles Times,* 18 March 1979, p. 70.

p. 51: *"...from the family."*: R. Kotlowitz, *Show: The Magazine of the Arts,* December 1964, p. 39.

II. THE PATH TO FANCY FREE 1940–1944

p. 53: *"...chance at a job."*: Jerome Robbins, introduction written in January 1996 for audiotape interview with E. Sorrin, Oral History Project, Dance Collection, Library of the Performing Arts at Lincoln Center, New York City, 28 November 1995.

p. 54: *only fourteen dancers were chosen.*: Hal Eaton, "Jerry Robbins Soared to Success By Bringing Ballet Down to Earth," *Long Island Press,* 10 July 1949, p. Q16.

p. 54: *count like a whiz.*: Agnes de Mille in "Dance Magazine's 1957 Awards: The Presentation," *Dance Magazine,* March 1958, p. 69.

p. 54: *"...stopped the show."*: Ibid.

p. 54: *"casts of thousands"*: Jerome Robbins, interview with Rosamond Bernier for WNET/*Dance in America,* New York City, 25 June 1986.

p. 54: *"too raunchy"*: Jerome Robbins, videotape interview with Deborah Jowitt, Kennedy Center Honors Oral History Program, 11 July 1995.

p. 55: *"...attending at the time."*: J. Robbins, interview with R. Bernier, 25 June 1986.

p. 60: *"...and not the misses."*: J. Robbins, interview with C. Barnes, 1973.

p. 61: *interesting formation of planes.*: Janet Reed in "A Fanfare for Jerome Robbins," *Ballet Review,* Summer 1988, p. 19.

p. 61: *"...first-rate invention to boot."*: John Martin, "Ballet by Robbins Called Smash Hit," *The New York Times,* 19 April 1944, p. 27.

p. 61: *"...one of those things."*: John Martin, "The Dance: 'Fancy Free' Does It," *The New York Times,* 23 April 1944, sect. 2, p. 8.

p. 63: *"...that's just for starters."*: Anna Kisselgoff, "The Dybbuk is Not Fancy Free," *The New York Times*, 12 May 1974, sect. 2, p. 3.

p. 71: *"...a drop of water."*: Lee Rogow, "Hottest Thing in Show Business," *Esquire,* November 1948, p. 125.

p. 75: *"...who was unknown then."*: J. Robbins, interview with R. Bernier, 25 June 1986.

p. 75: *"...I used ours."*: T. Tobias interview in *Dance Magazine,* January 1980, p. 69.

p. 76: *"...during the entire trip."*: J. Robbins, interview with R. Bernier, 25 June 1986.

p. 77: This graph is from *Dance Magazine,* May 1945.

p. 78: *"...from out of town."*: T. Tobias interview in *Dance Magazine,* January 1980, p. 69.

p. 81: *"...all the wrong things."*: J. Robbins, interview with R. Bernier, 25 June 1986.

p. 82: *"...their name to Robbins."*: R. Kotlowitz, *Show: The Magazine of the Arts,* December 1964, p. 39.

III. EARLY BALLET: BREAKING THE MOLD 1944–1957

p. 85: *"'...will be a masterpiece.'"*: Bernard Taper, *Balanchine: A Biography* (New York: Times Books, 1984; rpt. Berkeley, Calif.: Univ. of California Press, 1984), p. 230.

p. 86: *opinions on all subjects.*: T. Tobias interview in *Dance Magazine,* January 1980, p. 76.

p. 86: *"...to buy a ticket."*: Ibid.

p. 86: *"suddenly being thrown"*: Ibid.

p. 86: *change in status.*: Ibid.

p. 86: *"...successfully or not."*: John S. Wilson, "Robbins Turns to the Serious," *PM,* 24 October 1946, p. 18.

p. 86: *"...work with that company."*: J. Robbins, videotape interview with D. Jowitt, 11 July 1995.

p. 86: *...Balanchine said, "Come."*: Jerome Robbins, "A Conversation with Jerome Robbins: Working with Balanchine," videotape interview with Ellen Sorrin, New York City Ballet Guild Seminar, New York State Theater, 8 March 1993.

p. 87: *"...any choreographer to learn."*: Clive Barnes, "Ballet, Broadway and a Birthday," *Dance and Dancers,* June 1989, p. 16.

p. 89: *"...top of the material"*: J. Robbins, interview with C. Barnes, 1973.

p. 89: *truly satisfying comic ballets.*: D. Jowitt, *The New York Times Magazine,* 8 December 1974, p. 100.

p. 92: *"...must go off alone."*: J. S. Wilson, *PM,* 24 October 1946, p. 18.

p. 97: *"...what they are saying?"*: R. Sabin, *Dance Magazine,* August 1955, p. 23.

p. 99: *"...he was right."*: J. Robbins, videotape interview with E. Sorrin, 8 March 1993.

p. 100: *"...having to defend yourself."*: John Percival, "The Story Develops," *The London Times,* 30 June 1984, p. 19.

p. 103: *"...went like a dream."*: J. Robbins, videotape interview with D. Jowitt, 11 July 1995.

p. 107: *"...them back to earth."*: Jerome Robbins, "The Evolution of Modern Ballet," *World Theatre,* Winter 1959-60, p. 319.

p. 108: *"...structure which is satisfying."*: J. Robbins, interview with R. Bernier, 25 June 1986.

IV. EARLY BROADWAY: MASTERING THE CRAFT 1944–1957

p. 111: *"...me make The Concert."*: "Robbins: Back to Broadway": John Guare interview in *The New York Times Magazine,* 11 September 1988, p. 78.

p. 112: *"...It was lacerating."*: Angelica Gibbs, "Young Man from a Sad Generation," *Junior Bazaar,* April 1947, p. 138.

p. 112: *more personal subject matter*: E. Roberts, *Boston Post Magazine,* 8 May 1948, p. 15.

p. 115: *"...as well as it did."*: Frances Herridge, "Across the Footlights," *The New York Post,* 6 January 1958, p. 47.

p. 119: *"...women in the Forties."*: A. Gibbs, *Junior Bazaar,* April 1947, p. 136.

p. 123: *"...was a good one."*: J. Robbins, interview with C. Barnes, 1973.

p. 124: *"...call it dance movement."*: J. S. Wilson, *PM,* 24 October 1946, p. 18.

p. 127: *"...to give it emphasis."*: Selma Robinson, "Look, Ma, I'm An Autobiography!," *PM Sunday Magazine,* 21 December 1947, p. M8.

p. 129: *"...that they liked it."*: Sally MacDougall, "Choreographer's First Love–Cooking," *New York World-Telegram,* 22 November 1949, p. 21.

p. 131: *"...going to turn out."*: Phillip Bloom, "'Miss Liberty' Dances for Jerome Robbins," *Daily Compass,* 4 July 1949, p. 18.

p. 133: *"...devil is a choreographer?"*: Marie Torre, "Famed Dancer Shuns Hollywood," *New York World-Telegram,* 25 July 1959.

p. 135: *"...very helpful, and decisive."*: C. Barnes, *Dance and Dancers,* June 1989, p. 16.

p. 145: *"...but not by Hollywood."*: Walter Terry, "Robbins First Love," *New York Herald Tribune,* 8 October 1961, sect. 4, p. 6.

p. 151: *"...gesture of the show."*: Jerome Robbins in "Dramatist Guild Landmark Symposium on West Side Story," *Dramatist Guild Quarterly,* Autumn 1985, p. 25.

p. 151: *"...important and extraordinary time."* : Ibid., p. 14.

p. 152: "'...a wonderful idea here.'": Ibid., p. 11.

p. 152: "...on the West Side.": J. Percival, *The London Times,* 3 June 1984, p. 19.

p. 155: "...I think it should be.": M. Rothstein, *The New York Times,* 19 February 1989, sect. 2, page 14.

p. 158: "...like anything about it.": J. Robbins, videotape interview with D. Jowitt, 11 July 1995.

p. 158: "...of work on it.": J. Robbins, *Dramatist Guild Quarterly,* Autumn 1985, p. 14.

p. 162: "...no one ever did.": Jack Anderson, "Jerome Robbins, Pathbreaker," *The New York Times,* Sect. 2, 10 February 1985, p. 1.

V. CULMINATION:
THE MERGING OF DANCE AND STORY
1957–1965

p. 169: "...don't want to do.": John Corry, "Robbins Weighs the Future–Ballet or Broadway?," *The New York Times,* 12 July 1981, sect. 2, p. 20.

p. 170: *did not guarantee a hit.*: Ibid.

p. 170: *"extravagantly"*: Ibid.

p. 170: *...involved in filming a musical*: E. Coleman, *The New York Times Magazine,* 8 October 1961, p. 32.

p. 172: "...development in dance.": Jerome Robbins, "The Background of Ballets: U.S.A.," *Ballet Today,* Vol. 12, No. 8, October 1959, p. 12.

p. 175: "...choreography leads to.": M. Hunt, *Dance Magazine,* September 1997, p. 44.

p. 177: "...in silence...called Moves.": J. Robbins, interview with R. Bernier, 25 June 1986.

p. 183: "...renewing, refreshing.": W. Terry, *New York Herald Tribune,* 8 October 1961, sect. 4, p. 6.

p. 193: "'...to do another one?'": Jerome Robbins, as told to author.

p. 195: "...Beware of that.": J. Robbins, videotape interview with D. Jowitt, 11 July 1995.

p. 200: "...life through her children.": "Soup with Robbins," *The New Yorker,* 4 April 1959, p. 32.

p. 205: "...wasn't there originally.": C. Barnes, *Dance and Dancers,* June 1989, p. 17.

p. 207: "...to the present day.": Stuart W. Little, "Robbins Casts Middle-Aged Dancers," *New York Herald Tribune,* 11 June 1964, p. 12.

p. 207: *favorites in the show.*: R. Kotlowitz, *Show: The Magazine of the Arts,* December 1964, p. 40.

p. 208: "...background that I have.": J. Robbins, videotape interview with D. Jowitt, 11 July 1995.

VI. CHANGING COURSE:
A FERTILE NEW ERA   1965–1989

p. 211: "...pressure of the theater.": M. Rothstein, *The New York Times,* 19 February 1989, sect. 2, p. 15.

p. 212: "...[he] would a ballet": J. Corry, *The New York Times,* 12 July 1981, sect. 2, p. 20.

p. 212: *unending rehearsal*: Ibid.

p. 212: "...ever done, bar none.": D. Jowitt, *The New York Times Magazine,* 8 December 1974, p. 98.

p. 217: Clipping from *The New York Times,* 2 July 1978.

p. 218: "...inside of myself.": J. Robbins, videotape interview with E. Sorrin, 8 March 1993.

p. 223: "...problems of today?": J. Robbins, *World Theatre,* Winter 1959-60, p. 315.

p. 226: "...used to make them.": C. Barnes, *Dance and Dancers,* June 1989, p. 15.

p. 232: "...relationships with people.": Anna Kisselgoff, "Jerome Robbins: A Creator From Head to Foot," *The New York Times,* 3 June 1990, sect. 2, p. 6.

p. 235: "...that was the beginning.": D. Jowitt, *The New York Times Magazine,* 8 December 1974, p. 32.

p. 236: "...showed it to Balanchine.": J. Robbins, videotape interview with D. Jowitt, 11 July 1995.

p. 236: "'...You gotta do more.'": J. Robbins, videotape interview with E. Sorrin, 8 March 1993.

p. 238: "...so touched by that.": Ibid.

p. 240: "...no names for anything.": A. Kisselgoff, *The New York Times,* 3 June 1990, sect. 2, p. 1.

p. 246: "...a big dramatic thing": J. Robbins, videotape interview with D. Jowitt, 11 July 1995.

p. 251: "...as if I do.": Ibid.

p. 252: "'...enter the other world.'": J. Robbins, interview with R. Bernier, 25 June 1986.

p. 255: "...through to get there.": E. Coleman, *The New York Times Magazine,* 8 October 1961, p. 30.

p. 260: "...to lose those works.": J. Guare interview, *The New York Times Magazine,* 11 September 1988, p. 78.

VII. LAST BOWS   1990–1998

p. 265: "...going to try me.'": M. Rothstein, *The New York Times,* 19 February 1889, sect. 2, page 15.

p. 289: "...Because they will last.": D. Jowitt, *The New York Times Magazine,* 8 December 1974, p. 109.

p. 289: "...those of my dancers.": W. Terry, *New York Herald Tribune,* 8 October 1961, sect. 4, p. 6.

PERMISSIONS

Grateful acknowledgment is made to the following
for permission to reprint previously published and
unpublished material:

Clive Barnes: Excerpts from interview with Jerome
Robbins, New York City, 1973.

Rosamond Bernier: Excerpts from interview with Jerome
Robbins for WNET/*Dance in America,* New York City, 25
June 1986.

Dance Magazine: Jerome Robbins' graph for *Fancy Free*
(May 1945) and his photographs of *Moves* (June 1961).

The Kennedy Center for the Performing Arts: Excerpts
from videotape interview of Jerome Robbins by Deborah
Jowitt for Kennedy Center Honors Oral History Program,
11 July 1995.

The New York Historical Society: Endpaper maps, which
are Plates 83 and 76 in *Manhattan Land Book* (New York:
G.W. Bromley & Co., 1955). Collection of the New York
Historical Society. Reprinted with permission.

The New York Public Library: Lisa Parnova flyer and
review, Ballet Theatre contract, *Fancy Free* ad, *Look,
Ma, I'm Dancin'!* clipping (*PM,* 1947), *Two's Company* ad,
West Side Story clipping and *Gypsy* clipping.

The New York Times: Excerpts from articles by Jack
Anderson, Clive Barnes, Emily Coleman, John Corry,
John Guare, Deborah Jowitt, Anna Kisselgoff, John
Martin, Mervyn Rothstein, in addition to *Bells Are Ringing*
clipping and article about Jerome Robbins' dog Nick.
Copyright 1944, 1956, 1961, 1974, 1978, 1981, 1985, 1988,
1989, 1990, 1998 by The New York Times Company.
Reprinted with permission.

The Jerome Robbins Collection, Dance Division, the
New York Public Library at Lincoln Center: Fourteen pages
from Jerome Robbins' personal journals, as well as a
collage and one page of notes related to *Poppa Piece.*

Philip Lanza Sandor: Two Gluck-Sandor Dance Center
programs. Collection of Gluck-Sandor, courtesy of Philip
Lanza Sandor.

Ellen Sorrin and The New York Public Library at Lincoln
Center: Excerpts from audiotape interview for Dance
Collection Oral History Project (28 November 1995)
and videotape interview from New York City Ballet
Guild Seminar (8 March 1993), both conducted with
Jerome Robbins.

Saul Steinberg and the Jerome Robbins Collection
at the New York Public Library at Lincoln Center: Drop
created by Saul Steinberg for *The Concert,* 1958.

INDEX OF PHOTOGRAPHY

CHAPTER I
PAGES 25, 26, 28-31, 34-37 (all): The Jerome Robbins Collection, Dance Division, New York Public Library (hereafter JRC). PAGES 32, 33: Collection of Sonia Cullinen. PAGES 38-40 (all): Photographs by Lewis Goren/JRC. PAGE 41: Photograph by Lewis Goren/ Courtesy Tamiment Institute. PAGE 43: Photograph by Maurice Goldberg/Dance Division, Astor, Lenox and Tilden Foundations, New York Public Library (hereafter NYPL). PAGE 47: Photograph by Richard Oliver/JRC. PAGE 49: Photograph by Arnold Chekov/Gift of Freyman/ © Museum of the City of New York (hereafter MCNY). PAGE 50: Gift of Anna Teitlebaum Skulnik/ © MCNY. PAGE 51: Gift of Svee Schooler/© MCNY.

CHAPTER II
PAGE 52: Photograph by Richard Tucker/NYPL. PAGE 55: NYPL. PAGES 56-57: Photograph by Jerome Robinson/JRC. PAGE 62: Photograph by Constantine/ JRC. PAGES 66-67, 69-73 (all): JRC. PAGE 68: Photograph by Fred Fehl/JRC. PAGE 74: Photograph by Loomis Dean/TimePix. PAGE 79: Photograph by Kosti Ruohomaa, Black Star/NYPL. PAGES 80, 82-83: Photographs by Fred Fehl/NYPL.

CHAPTER III
PAGE 84: Photograph by Fred Fehl/New York City Ballet. PAGE 87: Photograph by Walter E. Owen/NYPL. PAGE 88: Photograph by George Platt Lynes/NYPL. PAGES 90-91, 100, 101: Photographs by Philippe Halsman/Courtesy Halsman Estate. PAGE 92: Photograph by George Karger/ JRC. PAGES 93, 104-105, 109: NYPL. PAGES 94-96 (all): Photofest/NYPL. PAGES 98-99, 106, 107: Photographs by Fred Fehl/NYPL. PAGE 102: Photograph by Melton-Pippin/NYPL.

CHAPTER IV
PAGE 110: Photograph by Philippe Halsman/Courtesy Halsman Estate. PAGES 113, 114, 116, 120-121, 125, 137: © Eileen Darby/Darby Collection. PAGE 117: © MCNY, 1944. PAGES 122-123: © Eileen Darby/TimePix. PAGE 126: Archive Photos. PAGE 127: Photograph by Warnecke & Schoenbaechler/NYPL. PAGE 128-129: Photofest/NYPL. PAGE 130: © MCNY, 1949. PAGES 132-133: Photograph by George Karger/TimePix. PAGES 134, 135: © MCNY, 1950. PAGE 138: Photograph by Will Rapport/NYPL. PAGES 140, 142-144 (all), 146-147: Photofest. PAGE 150: Photograph by Alfred Eisenstaedt/TimePix.

PAGES 153 top, 164-167 (all): Photographs by Fred Fehl/ © MCNY, 1957. PAGES 153 bottom, 154, 156-157, 159-161 (all): Photographs by Martha Swope/TimePix. PAGES 162, 163: © Eileen Darby/Darby Collection.

CHAPTER V
PAGES 168, 174-175, 186-189 (all): Photographs by Philippe Halsman/Courtesy Halsman Estate. PAGES 171, 173, 183: Photographs by Martha Swope/TimePix. PAGES 172, 201: NYPL. PAGES 174-175: Photographs by Jerome Robbins/ NYPL. PAGES 178, 191, 194, 197-199 (all): Photofest. PAGES 180-181: Photograph by Martha Swope/Photofest. PAGE 182: Photograph by Radford Bascome/NYPL. PAGES 190, 192-193: Photographs by Richard Wyatt/ NYPL. PAGE 196: © Academy of Motion Picture Arts & Sciences. PAGES 202-209 (all): Billy Rose Theater Collection, New York Public Library.

CHAPTER VI
PAGES 214, 215: Photographs by Jesse Gerstein/JRC. PAGE 216: Women's Wear Daily/Fairchild Publications. PAGE 227: Photograph by Friedman-Abeles/Photofest. PAGES 228, 229, 236-238 (all): Photographs by Gjon Mili/ TimePix. PAGE 231: Photograph © Dominique Nabokov. PAGES 232-235 (all), 239-245 (all), 246 left, 248-251 (all), 253, 254, 256-257, 260-263 (all): Photographs by Martha Swope/TimePix. PAGE 246 right: Photograph by Henry Grossman/TimePix. PAGE 247: NYPL. PAGES 258-259: Photograph © Steve Caras.

CHAPTER VII
PAGES 264, 267, 268: JRC. PAGES 270-271: Photograph by Ted Thai/TimePix. PAGES 272, 273, 282-285 (all): Photographs © Paul Kolnik. PAGES 274-275, 288: Photographs by Costas. PAGES 280-281: Photograph by Danielle Freedman/JRC.

INDEX

Page numbers in *italics* refer to the illustrations

ABOUT THE AUTHOR

Christine Conrad has had a rich and varied career in movies, theater, publishing and New York City politics. Her numerous screenplays for motion pictures and television include *Junior,* the comedy starring Arnold Schwarzenegger, Danny DeVito and Emma Thompson. A renowned advocate for women's health, she founded the Natural Woman Institute, and her books include *A Woman's Guide to Natural Hormones* and, with Dr. Marcus Laux, the best-selling *Natural Woman, Natural Menopause.* Ms. Conrad resides in Los Angeles, California.

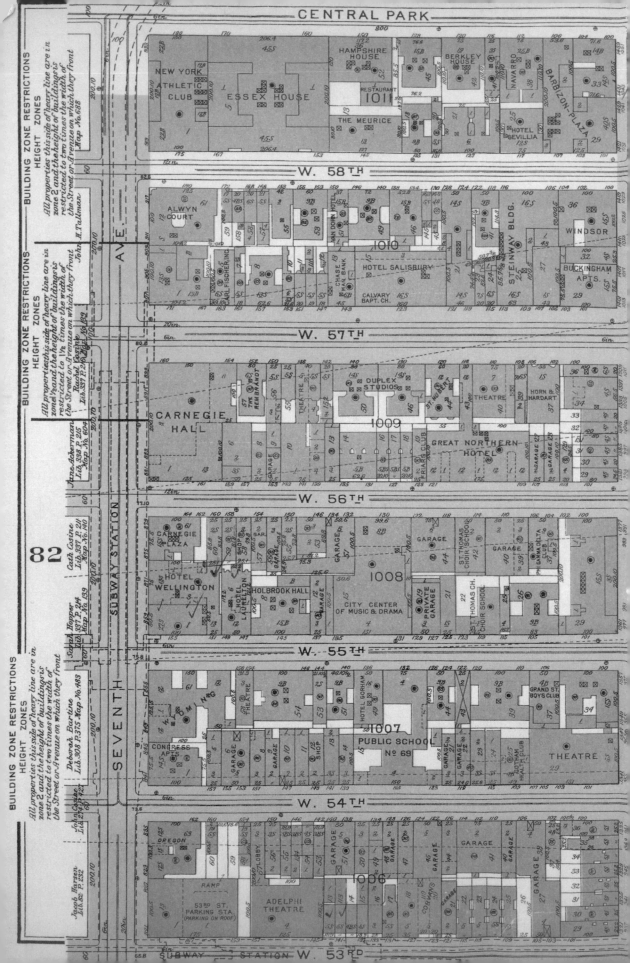